LIGHTS, CAMERA, HISTORY

NUMBER FORTY:
The Walter Prescott Webb Memorial Lectures

LIGHTS, CAMERA, HISTORY
PORTRAYING THE PAST IN FILM

. . . .

EDITED BY RICHARD FRANCAVIGLIA
AND JERRY RODNITZKY

With an Introduction by
   Peter C. Rollins

Contributions by
   Robert Rosenstone
   Geoff Pingree
   Richard Francaviglia
   Daniel A. Nathan
   Peter Berg
   Erin Klemyk
   Robert Brent Toplin

Published for the University of Texas at Arlington by

TEXAS A&M UNIVERSITY PRESS
College Station

LIBRARY OF CONGRESS CATALOGING-IN-PUBLICATION DATA

Lights, camera, history : portraying the past in film / edited by Richard
Francaviglia and Jerry Rodnitzky ; with an Introduction by Peter C.
Rollins ; contributions by Robert Rosenstone . . . [et al.].—1st ed.
    p.   cm.—(The Walter Prescott Webb memorial lectures ; no. 40)
Includes bibliographical references.
ISBN-13: 978-1-58544-566-0 (cloth : alk. paper)
ISBN-10: 1-58544-566-5 (cloth : alk. paper)
ISBN-13: 978-1-58544-580-6 (pbk. : alk. paper)
ISBN-10: 1-58544-580-0 (paper : alk. paper)
1. Motion pictures and history.   2. Historical films—History and
criticism.   I. Francaviglia, Richard V.   II. Rodnitzky, Jerome L.,
1936–   III. Rosenstone, Robert A.
PN1995.2.L54 2007
791.43'658—dc22

                                            2006021746

CONTENTS

....

To friend and colleague Gerald Saxon

PREFACE

····

RICHARD FRANCAVIGLIA & JERRY RODNITZKY

As editors, we are delighted to present these essays from the 2005 Walter Prescott Webb Lectures. The Webb Lectures, which are annually presented at the University of Texas at Arlington, have a long history. The year 2005, in fact, marked the fortieth anniversary of this lecture series. The theme in 2005 provided our university with the opportunity to explore a subject that has interested us for many years: how history is depicted in popular film. As historians, we've often watched films that attempt to capture the past. However, we have just as often wondered what has been lost, and what has been gained, when filmmakers interpret that history.

The Webb Lectures answered many of those questions and posed just as many new ones. The lectures reaffirmed something else of importance to history and film studies—the concept of accuracy in light of larger truths. Almost any historian can reel off lists of inaccuracies in films like *Cleopatra, Pearl Harbor,* or *JFK*. Historians have long noted with interest, and even delight, the fact that although filmmakers often strive for accuracy, something usually compromises their ability to get their facts right (assuming, of course, that all the facts are known). That, perhaps, is because filmmakers often succumb to the temptation to tell *their own* stories. This not only makes such films autobiographical, it often makes them extremely controversial—to historians at least.

It might be easy, then, to simply dismiss film as a hopeless medium for relating history, but we refuse to do so for at least three reasons. The first relates to the largely unexplored *potential* of films to convey the intensity and complexity of history. That belief may reveal our inherent optimism, but we hope historians will not shy away from using the medium for a second reason, namely because film itself is such a good medium for *teaching* history—and controversies about it—in the classroom. If you are the kind of historian who bemoans the treatment of your favorite historical subject at the hands of scriptwriters, directors, and editors, then it is your responsibility to employ that medium: write, script, or direct a film yourself; hopefully, it will be better than much of what you and your students see on-screen. More likely, you will highlight the inaccuracies and accuracies of films as you teach from them, but we hope you will also recognize what the films achieve as well as how they fail. This is clearly what the contributors to this volume have attempted. If you are a historian who dismisses film as a serious teaching tool, think again. If you don't use films, your students will. Our current students are clearly a film generation. Increasingly, they see more films and read fewer books. And around the world, even young people who distrust or even hate the United States as the one remaining superpower are increasingly mesmerized by American films.

Our third reason for refusing to dismiss historically themed films relates to what some see as an inherent flaw in the medium—namely, its ability to emotionalize history. Here we urge historians to recognize that a filmmaker can help *create* emotions anew—elation, anger, despair, grief, fear—that may have characterized historical periods. In this sense, film's power to emotionalize by engaging the viewer offers the potential to tell stories—that is, interpret the historical record—in new and exciting ways like no other medium.

We believe that the Fortieth Walter Prescott Webb Lectures were successful in many ways. They helped the attendees understand and imagine new uses for film in historical interpretation. Regardless of your personal feelings about historically themed films, then, we invite you to read these varied essays with a view toward better understanding this inescapable medium.

LIGHTS, CAMERA, HISTORY

INTRODUCTION
FILM AND HISTORY: OUR MEDIA
ENVIRONMENT AS A NEW FRONTIER
····

PETER C. ROLLINS

Contemporary Americans know what they know about foreign affairs, domestic politics, and history primarily from what they see on the motion picture screen, television, and—in a recycled form—on videotape and DVD technologies. The latter bring classic fiction films and documentaries to homes as rental items or purchases, blurring the distinction between movie attendance and home entertainment. These developments in access to television and film are simultaneously a threat to our culture and a boon to educators. It is up to us, in fact, to grasp the challenge and to devise ways in which to make these entertainment media work to enhance our popular memory. Back in 1970, John O'Connor and Martin A. Jackson saw this challenge looming on the intellectual horizon. In response, they founded a journal entitled *Film & History: An Interdisciplinary Journal of Film and Television History* (www.filmand history.org). That journal has passed through various hands over the last thirty-five years, but it has addressed many of the issues that are explored in this fine collection of essays. The main purpose of this book is to shed light on the fascinating, and sometimes troubling, subject of how films interpret history. The five essays in this collection explore significant frontier trails for film/history studies.

In the first essay, "In Praise of the Biopic," Robert Rosenstone addresses a persistent theme—*the way in which film treats controversial events in history*. In describing how the film *Reds* treated Jack Reed's involvement with the Communist Party, Rosenstone reminds us that it is impossible to separate a film from its own place in social history. Then, too, there is always the filmmaker's agenda. Whether they tell the story of great leaders or ordinary people, motion pictures put their spin on history. Custer's "last stand" was a high moment of courage in the pre-WWII film *They Died with Their Boots On* (1941, starring Errol Flynn), yet the same story later became an example of personal hubris and national arrogance in the Vietnam-era *Little Big Man* (1970, starring Dustin Hoffman). The Errol Flynn version saw a heroic expansion of white civilization into a savage wilderness, while the Dustin Hoffman perspective questioned, during the Vietnam conflict, the right of Americans to invade and acquire lands not their own. More recently, both *Seabiscuit* (2003) and *Cinderella Man* (2005) portray the Great Depression in a manner that celebrates the power of individuals to triumph over nearly overwhelming conditions. Both films give a hopeful interpretation on the impact of the era on ordinary citizens; not everyone was destroyed by the nationwide setbacks of that crucial decade, John Ford's *The Grapes of Wrath* (1941) notwithstanding.

The second essay, by Geoff Pingree, is titled "History Is What Remains: Cinema's Challenge to Ideas about the Past." In it, Pingree asks very broad questions about the nature of history and historical interpretation, focusing on Jay Rosenblatt's *History Remains* (1998). Explored are basic questions about historical documents as texts, the nature of historical "truth," and how differently readers/viewers relate to verbal and visual messages. Here, Pingree calls attention to the creative talent needed to write history and/or to produce cinematic interpretations of the past. In a review of the film included in the press kit, noted scholar Ernest Giglio has urged that "*History Remains* will prove to be a valuable classroom resource. No viewer will leave the film unchanged." To question the very nature of documents is also to question the insights to be gained via documentary film; *Human Remains* thus becomes a thirty-minute Rorschach training ground for classes discussing historical method. (The film won a Jury Award at the Sundance Film Festival, a major coup for any film.) Those interested in such object lessons for exegesis should consider two other very successful pedagogical films: *Goodbye Billy: America Goes to War, 1917-1918* (1970, Cadre Films) and *Will Rogers' 1920s: A Cowboy's Guide to the Times* (1976, Cadre Films). Both have been discussed at length by the filmmakers in the pages of *Film & History*.

The third essay, "Crusaders and Saracens: The Persistence of Orientalism in Historically Themed Motion Pictures about the Middle East," traces a pervasive theme in Western perceptions of the Orient. Richard Francaviglia applies the concept of "Orientalism" (and, conversely, Occidentalism) to both cultural history and to a rather broad spectrum of major motion pictures from Howard Hughes's unconvincing *The Conqueror* (1956) to more recent productions such as Joe Johnson's *Hidalgo* (2004) and Ridley Scott's *Kingdom of Heaven* (2005). Francaviglia argues that negative—indeed, antipathetic—stereotypes about the East pervade Western culture; these simplified codes are then exaggerated by screenwriters to suit the dramatic needs of motion pictures. After 9/11 (USA) and 7/7 (UK) terrorist crises, every citizen of the globe needs to be aware of cultural prejudices and their implications. As Edward Said wrote, "The Orient was almost a European invention, and had been since antiquity a place of romance, exotic beings, haunted memories and landscapes, remarkable experiences—that now form part of a colonial discourse with the eastern world." That is true, but Francaviglia also observes that Orientalism involves considerable appreciation of Eastern cultures—and that exposure to the East can reorient, in Francaviglia's words, the Westerner's viewpoint. Teachers are urged to study the method of this essay, as it explores details of real history in relation to the reports of the reel history.

The fourth essay, "'The Truth Wrapped in a Package of Lies': Hollywood, History, and Martin Scorsese's *Gangs of New York*" examines Martin Scorsese's critically acclaimed *Gangs of New York* (2002) with a historical magnifying glass. Authors David A. Nathan, Peter Berg, and Erin Klemyk see many virtues in this historical film about the 1863 draft riots in New York City, arguing that it is an intellectually complex interpretation of the immigrant experience. Even invented scenes in *Gangs of New York* are praised for their evocation of historical truth. The Tammany Hall political machine, the class chasms and conflicts, the racial antagonisms were all part of the city's experience, and Scorsese is given high marks for vividly bringing these social tensions to the screen. According to the authors of this essay, "*Gang's* greatest accomplishment . . . is its emotional force, its ability to communicate the texture and furor of the past." Implicit in their interpretation of the historical value of the epic film is the assumption that the analysts' own interests in race, class, and gender have been overlooked by historians. Our young scholars are often excited to find their interests reflected in new motion pictures.

The fifth essay in this volume, "In Defense of the Filmmakers" by Robert Brent Toplin, directly addresses the second point that I would like to discuss in this introduction that is also a major subtext in this book, namely, *that (and how) films reflect history.* Before discussing Toplin's essay in some detail, however, I would like to place his work in both historic context and in the context of the Webb Lectures.

It is often the case that motion pictures reflect the attitudes of their time—often unconsciously. The sound-era films of Will Rogers—feature productions such as *David Harem* (1934), *In Old Kentucky* (1935), and

Steamboat 'Round the Bend (1935)—were written and produced as what is often described as "pure entertainment." Those of us who study motion pictures in a cultural context see more in these productions: as a film icon, Will Rogers appealed to a strong longing for a nineteenth-century, rural-based, community-oriented society that had been destroyed by the industrial age. As the Great Depression deepened, many Americans became wistful for the pre-1900 years when people lived—at least as viewed retrospectively—in an era of *gemeinschaft*. The popularity of these rural fantasies says much about the rejection of modernity under the pressures of hard times. But one thing is clear: these escapes into the 1890s were a reflection of the inner spiritual life of the 1930s.

The genre approach to film (i.e., war film, western film, musical film) has shown that generic conventions evolve over time as the preoccupations of filmmakers and audiences change. Even the work of particular filmmakers evolves, reflecting changing attitudes. For example, in 1939 John Ford's *Stagecoach* told the story of civilization vs. the wilderness in a manner that could have been endorsed by the most ardent advocate of Manifest Destiny. Yet, by the end of his career, in *The Searchers* (1956) and *Cheyenne Autumn* (1964) this great director revised his sanguine vision of white expansion into Indian territory. His *Sergeant Rutledge* (1960) condemned the evils of racism during the height of civil rights activism. Yet all of these films were Westerns; the changes in plot, characterization, setting, and theme reflected the evolution of an artist's sensibility and a nation's conscience.

This subject has an international dimension. Francaviglia's essay addresses this issue by identifying the pervasiveness of Orientalism in European and American thinking and then traces how this view of the East (i.e., the Middle East), as a result, has been a basic organizational principle for such popular films as *Lawrence of Arabia* (1962), *Conan the Barbarian* (1982), *True Lies* (1994)—even the *Lord of the Rings* trilogy (2001–3). As they provide entertainment their vision is often distorted by deep-seated negative attitudes about the Oriental "other." Yet, as Francaviglia shows, we are ambivalent about the East, and our films reveal that ambivalence.

Another theme worth mentioning in this introduction—but not discussed much in these essays—is that *films attempt to influence history itself.* If we think about this carefully, we can recognize countless examples of motion pictures made to influence their times. During World War II, Frank Capra—the Academy Award–winning director of *It Happened One Night* (1934) and *Mr. Deeds Goes to Town* (1936)—was called to Washington to produce a series of "orientation films" for troops headed overseas. The *Why We Fight* series he developed consisted of eight hour-long films designed to erase the last vestiges of isolationism in the minds of troops,

PETER C. ROLLINS

especially those from the American heartland (Iowa, Kansas, Okla-homa, Texas), the breadbasket of isolationism. In addition, by showing the brutality of the Axis enemies and the scope of their global objectives, the films fostered a fighting spirit that would lead to victory. In recent times, Michael Moore has made a number of documentaries designed to change history: *Roger and Me* (1989) is his critique of America's big corporations and their lack of compassion; *Bowling for Columbine* (2002) tried to show that America's gun culture—with the help of a villainized Charlton Heston—was responsible for a national tragedy; *Fahrenheit 9/11* was an explicit effort to influence a presidential election in 2004 by showing the putative mendacity and greed of the Bush family and for-mer Halliburton CEO Dick Cheney. There is a long list of films and film-makers intent on influencing the American demos. In such discussions, the name of director Oliver Stone is bound to be mentioned.

In this collection there is less emphasis on films designed to sway audiences because so much attention has been devoted to the represen-tation of the past, but some examples discussed are worthy of mention. Consider again, for example, Robert Rosenstone's considerably detailed discussion of the film *Reds*. No doubt Warren Beatty, in making *Reds*, was attempting to connect the international saga of radicalism to an American setting. This is powerfully embodied in the career of John Reed, one of the few Americans buried in the Kremlin, but also rein-forced by interviews edited into the film with American radicals who offer "witness" about their goals. Such a theme is close to Hollywood's heart and was in harmony with the activism of the 1960s and 1970s; that *Reds* appeared in the same year that Ronald Reagan moved into the White House made the film all the more important as a countercultural statement.

The historical romance *Walker* (1987) was seen as a belated condemna-tion of America's adventurism in Vietnam in the 1960s; the film contains an anachronistic reenactment of the evacuation of the Saigon Embassy in 1975—albeit placed in the 1840s at the end of Walker's reign in Nica-ragua. The director's strategic placement of deliberately anachronistic items from American culture—a Coca-Cola bottle and a *Time* magazine, for example—is a jarring reminder of the United States' involvement in the third world. Director Alex Cox was clearly using an eccentric case study in imperialism to editorialize about a recent American failure in southeastern Asia and the Reagan administration's putative adventur-ism in modern-day Nicaragua.

Now that I have set the scene, so to speak, I shall address Robert B. Toplin's contribution to this collection of essays. As Toplin points out in his essay, one of the most negative films made to influence popular audiences was *The Birth of a Nation* (1915). It served as a major prop for the return of segregation in America during the otherwise progressive administration of Woodrow Wilson (1913–21). The film celebrated the heroic return to white dominance after the era of Reconstruction (1865–77). Its popularity continued in later years as the proud emblem of the Ku Klux Klan. (Every chapter of the illicit organization owned a print of the perverse epic.) Toplin also suggests (with others) that President Richard Nixon gained confidence in his strategic plans for the Vietnam War by watching George C. Scott portray a decisive *Patton* (1970). Basking in a cinematic afterglow, Nixon ordered the invasion of North Vietnamese sanctuaries in Cambodia, thereby setting off protests on campuses across the nation, most notably at Kent State in 1970, where four students were killed during the third day of protests.

All of the essays more or less address a major underlying issue about writing history—*accuracy vs. truth*. We know that many historians are dismissive of motion pictures because they manipulate facts, conflate historical characters, and communicate through symbols and microcosms rather than employ word-laden discursive techniques. Like many traditional scholars, historians are uncomfortable with visual language and—although influenced by it—have never studied the techniques and tricks filmmakers use to get their interpretations across to audiences.

In the first essay, Rosenstone defends a genre, the "biopic" (biographical film), in a manner that runs against the grain of existing scholarship, most notably George F. Custen's fascinating study, *Bio/Pics: How Hollywood Constructed Public History*. Custen's overview is highly critical of the biopic genre for representing the views of the filmmakers and studio executives more than those of the ostensible subjects of such "prestige pictures"—Louis Pasteur, Emile Zola, Alexander Graham Bell, and Marie Antoinette. Rather than being a detractor of the genre, Rosenstone—who completed an important biography of John Reed in 1975 and then served as historical advisor to Warren Beatty when that youthful actor directed (and starred in) *Reds*—argues that both authors and filmmakers must make a number of similar artistic decisions about their subjects. Each must cast the person into a story that includes both his personal life and the public life of the era; each must decide what incidents are to be examined in detail and what people are to be prominent to fulfill the story arc, including invented characters; finally, each will inevitably "invent" incidents that allow the artist—literary or cinematic—to evoke the inner truths about character.

Borrowing from Ira Nadel, Rosenstone suggests that biographies should subscribe to "Boswellian understanding rather than Baconian data." Some leading examples explored are John Ford's *Young Mr. Lincoln*

(1939), a film often criticized by Lincoln specialists and *Walker* (1987), a rendering of history that counts Rosenstone as a rare—albeit prestigious—admirer. As an expert on John Reed, Rosenstone examines three very different films about the young cheerleader for the Bolshevik Revolution and finds that each, due to a different approach, has its own insights. The real John Reed eludes all of them, but these biopics are valuable as historical interpretations: they are, in Rosenstone's words, more than pale reflections of some sterile "true history." In his support for films as "interpretations," Rosenstone is very much in agreement with Robert Brent Toplin.

Toplin's essay addresses the great paradox of film as an art form. While conceding that films have inherent weaknesses because of their visual mode and time constrictions, Toplin argues that historical interpretations in film have an impressive track record. For example, the television series *Holocaust* (1978) sparked discussion of that historical nightmare not only in the United States but also in Europe. Reviewers, scholars, and citizens were forced to reexamine the legacy of Nazi Germany and to discuss the evils of racism, clearly a heuristic exercise in all eras. In conjunction with the D-Day memorials, *Saving Private Ryan* (1998) stimulated an enormous market for monographs and oral histories focused on World War II. Tom Brokaw, in this context, coined a familiar term, "the greatest generation," which seems, unfortunately, to have been accepted as a basic concept of history rather than an honorific moniker bestowed by an admiring network reporter.

Toplin astutely notes that films set an emotional hook: "By engaging the audience's sympathies for principal characters, these movies arouse a hunger for greater knowledge about the historical context." For example, the Civil War film *Glory* (1989) portrays the New England regiment of African Americans as former slaves when, in fact, they were predominantly free citizens. James McPherson, a major scholar and former president of the American Historical Association, is cited as approving this distortion of fact because it better spoke to the African American military experience during the conflict: As Toplin observes, "The director (and screenwriter, Kevin Jarre) manipulated a small 'truth' in order to advance understanding of an important larger 'truth.'" The final thrust of Toplin's contribution aims in the direction one would expect from an educator. While no booster for Hollywood history, Toplin observes that "Hollywood movies do not bring closure to discussions about history. But," he concludes, "they do have the potential to open them."

This debate about artistic vs. historical truth is not new. In recent times, Oliver Stone has defended such controversial films as *JFK* and *Platoon* as a form of cinematic history. At great length, Stone has argued that, while distorting details of his stories as understood by historians, he has been after a "deeper" truth—as it were, a truth below mere surface facts. This debate about "facticity" is not a new one, and we commit a grave error to restrict it to the discussion of motion picture history. For those of us with a literary background, the debate about artistic vs. historical truth goes back to nineteenth-century discussions of the contrasting purposes of the "romance" as opposed to the "novel." In the various prefaces to his novels, Nathaniel Hawthorne argued that the artist studies history to discover truths of the human heart. To accomplish that end, the artist *must* distort and invent because mere facts often obscure important personal and corporate truths. The very first paragraph of Hawthorne's preface to *The House of the Seven Gables* (1851) would serve well as a defense of liberties taken by *conscientious* directors who render history into film:

> When a writer calls his work a Romance, it need hardly be observed that he wishes to claim a certain latitude, both as to its fashion and material, which he would not have felt himself entitled to assume, had he professed to be writing a Novel. The latter form of composition is presumed to aim at a very minute fidelity, not merely to the possible, but to the probable and ordinary course of man's experience. The former—while, as a work of art, it must rigidly subject itself to laws, and while it sins unpardonably, so far as it may swerve aside from the truth of the human heart—has fairly a right to present that truth under circumstances, to a great extent, of the writer's own choosing or creation.

The essays by Rosenstone and Toplin support this tolerance of license in the name of truth (rather than mere accuracy). With special skills in summing up this issue, Geoff Pingree describes the creative opportunity for all histories—written or cinematic: "So it is with history in film: that things happened, that events occurred, we can agree, but the problem is how we negotiate the distance that exists inevitably between us and these events and happenings." Here, indeed, is an opportunity for imagination to dredge meaning out of experience.

I shall conclude this introduction by noting that these essays' namesake—historian Walter Prescott Webb—would have been pleased with the work of the authors included in this collection. Like his mentor, Frederick Jackson Turner, Webb was concerned with historical method and particularly interested in the relationship between people and their environments. In our media age, it is essential for citizens to be aware of the power of motion pictures and television to determine our *media*

PETER C. ROLLINS

environment. The sheer duration of viewing each day by the ordinary American—as much as six hours—cannot be dismissed as "mere entertainment" because the popular arts entertain only when they touch audience anxieties and aspirations. In the process, they shape popular culture and, over time, popular perceptions.

By treating historical films as works of art, we can appreciate the productions as we keep alert to the interpretations imposed by cinematic artists. In doing so, we become visually literate and better able to understand our past—and, therefore, our responsibilities in the present. Students can be reached in this way, and they are our future. In the days of Turner, historians were overemphasizing the European roots of American institutions, and he stepped in to remind his colleagues about the influence of the frontier in American history. This collection, in studying the pitfalls and positive potentials for historical films, has further called attention to a scholarly frontier for our own time—the study of film and history.

·FOR FURTHER STUDY:

Peter C. Rollins, ed., *The Columbia Companion to American History on Film* (New York: Columbia University Press, 2003).
Film & History: An Interdisciplinary Journal of Film and Television History. www.filmandhistory.org

IN PRAISE OF THE BIOPIC

....

ROBERT ROSENSTONE

obody has ever had much good to say about the biographical film—a form usually dismissed with a kind of sneer as the "biopic." Though over the last forty years, fourteen of the Academy Awards for Best Picture have gone to such films, these have presumably been given for dramatic excellence rather than historical insight or truth. Critic Ronald Bergan expresses a kind of common wisdom when he writes (appropriating a line from Roland Barthes): "the biopic is a fiction that dare not speak its name . . . [it takes] people's real lives and transforms them into the realms of myth."[1] The only scholar to investigate the topic at length, George F. Custen, puts the negative case in stronger terms: "Hollywood biography is to history what Caesar's Palace is to architectural history: an enormous, engaging distortion, which after a time convinces us of its own kind of authenticity."[2]

These judgments refer to the products of Hollywood—those largely made in the era of the studio system—and ignore independent films or those shot in the rest of the world. Custen's book, *Bio/Pics*, focuses on the years 1927–60, though in a later essay he brings the study up to 1980.[3] If the subjects of biographical films change somewhat in the latter period, with the lives of more women and non-Americans depicted on-screen, the author finds little change in the overall shape and meaning of the form. The biopic is "based on the cosmology of the movie industry. . . . In this view of history, the greatness of the individual figure becomes that set of qualities that made a producer great or powerful in Hollywood rather than those traits that characterized the famous person in his or her own lifetime."[4]

One problem with this assertion is that while Custen deals extensively with the mores and practices of Hollywood, he never gets around to actually testing to what extent the latter half of it may be true—that is, he fails to place biopics into the larger discourse surrounding particular figures. Given his overall aim as a professor of communications, to chart the patterns of biopics over time, this is an understandable lapse. But this lapse is certain to leave unsatisfied anyone interested in the problems of shaping biography on film, of just how one can render a life—either in words on the page or in images on-screen (or in any other way). If Custen is uninterested in the contents of biography, Bergan takes a particularly narrow view of its traditions and practices. He warns that we should not go to the biopic "as we do to a literary biography, to learn the facts of lives under scrutiny."[5] But is that the reason we go to biographies—to learn the facts? Interesting as they may be, facts could be delivered with chronicles and lists of data. If facts were the aim, we would have no need of the literary form of the biography.

The life story, as set down in words on the page, has a history and a tradition. To begin to understand the biographical film—its shape and structure, the way it handles data, the way it creates the world in which its subject thinks and acts—one must attempt to see the form within the larger issues of biography. Clearly, to do biography is to make the case that individuals are either at the center of the historical process—or are worth studying as exemplars of lives, actions, and individual value systems we either admire or dislike or admire and dislike. But exactly how you do that has been a matter of debate as long as the telling of lives has been a literary endeavor—for more than two millennia in the West. Over this span of time, notions of the aims and purposes of biography have often shifted, and one looks in vain for some consensus across the ages. Is biography the story of great people (for most of history, men) we wish to emulate or great villains we wish to condemn? Should it focus on public life or (as more recently) personal life? Should it show its subject as a creature of the times or someone who rises above history and creates the times, or somehow split the difference and have it both ways?

Today, decades after literary theorists have turned their critical eyes upon the genre, little about biography has been settled—ultimately it is an elusive, perhaps even an undefinable, form. People who write biographies, and theorists too (many of the latter are also the former), have a great deal of trouble explaining in any systematic (or even unsystematic) way exactly what elements make for a good biography. To read much

ROBERT ROSENSTONE

in the field is to understand that biography possesses no hard and fast rules. The best you can say is that it is always a highly interpretive act, one that inevitably includes fictional components—here using "fiction" in its original meaning from Latin, in the sense of "formed." Yet many who write on the topic also admit that the genre often contains doses of fiction in the more modern sense of "an imaginative creation."

Roland Barthes put it simply, calling biography (in the phrase that Ronald Bergan lifted) "the fiction that dare not speak its name."[6] Others have elaborated on this insight. Carolyn Heilbrun asks, "Who can write a biography without inventing a life? A biographer, like a writer of fiction, imposes a pattern upon events, invents a protagonist, and discovers the pattern of his or her life."[7] Paula Backscheider expands upon this notion: "The best biographers know that they are inventing through their selection and arrangement of materials; they are establishing cause-effect and other relationships, and they are determining what was most formative and important for someone else, someone they do not know. They must choose what to include, leave out, emphasize, and subordinate, and when they do, they have constructed a narrative that, whether they are aware of it or not, partakes of cultural stories with expectations for resolutions and interpretations built in. . . . Narrative becomes the life and the basis for the judgments that will be rendered about the subject."[8]

It may seem surprising to start a discussion of biography with its fictional elements since common wisdom sees facts as the basis of a life. But the relationship between fact and the *story* of a life has always been tenuous and shifting. Too much fact, too many details, and you are likely to bury your subject by smothering the larger interpretive patterns that make us understand (or so we think) a life—as we can see by looking at the three- and four-volume lives that entombed so many nineteenth-century politicians, statesmen, and military leaders. True, the importance of fact in and to biography has grown over the last two centuries, paralleling the growth of empiricism in the human sciences as well as larger changes in the cultural and historical climate. Yet most theorists of the form understand, as Ira Nadel points out in *Biography: Fiction, Fact, and Form*, that facts alone cannot explain the configuration that constitutes a life. Often biographers depart from facts or bend them in order to create a particular atmosphere or mood or a more consistent figure of a historical person. The aim in such cases, which Nadel traces back to the 1830s, has been "Boswellian understanding rather than Baconian data."[9]

Ultimately the relationship between fact and fiction, content and form in biography becomes what Hayden White has called a problem of the writing: "we make sense of the world by imposing on it the formal coherency that we customarily associate with fiction." It is this fictive power that explains how bio translates fact into literary event. According to Nadel, "we resolve our own sense of fragmentation through the unity or story of the lives of others." [10] For him it is precisely this fictive story that provides us with a coherent vision of life.

Questions of the boundary lines between fact and fiction in the representation of past lives also mark the literature on the historical novel. Without making a major excursion into that field, I simply wish to draw on Sir Walter Scott, the major figure in the English language genre, for some insight into the problems of telling lives. Scott was an author who well understood that it was impossible to reproduce the past as it really had been, that part of his task involved a great deal of "translation" (his word) in order to make a long vanished world accessible to his audience. In the dedication to *Ivanhoe*, Scott confronts this question directly by explaining he is not, after all, writing in Anglo-Saxon or Norman French (the languages of the period in which the story is set) but in modern English—which is a first and basic sort of translation. But there are others as well. For example, it is impossible, Scott admits, to confine his vocabulary, ideas, and sense of life entirely within the limits of the time frame in which the story unfolds because part of his task is to convey this lost world to a modern audience: "It is necessary for exciting interest of any kind that the subject assumed should be, as it were, translated into the manners as well as the language, of the age we live in. . . . " [11]

The imposed fiction of a story, the creative use of fact, the translation necessary to make a life comprehensible and interesting—all these elements that are part of traditional biographical writing (and the historical novel) also mark the biographical film (where part of the translation involves the use of the visual media and sound). The latter, in short, belongs to a long tradition. What this means is that the written biography and the biographical film are less different than they may appear to be. The overall project of telling a life is similar in both media. Biographer and filmmaker both appropriate some of the trace details left by a life and weave them into a story whose theme infuses meaning into the days of their subject. The resulting work is ultimately based less on the raw data than on that data incorporated into a vision created by the literary (or filmic) skills of the biographer. That is why very different bios can be made about the life of the same individual, without any new data having been found. (Like the director of the historical film, the biographer on film also must "invent" fact to meet the double demands of the dramatic form and the time frame of film. For an explication of this, see my essay "Inventing Historical Truth on the Silver Screen.")[12]

As the major subgenre of the history film, the biofilm represents a large field. Custen enumerates 396 such works produced in Hollywood between 1927 and 1980. This is but the tip of a huge iceberg, for not only does his study omit the last quarter century, it wholly ignores works made in other parts of the world (including countries like Britain, Germany, France, Italy, and Japan, which have rich film traditions) and never mentions a single one of the vast number of biofilms that have been produced for television all over the globe in the last half century. Given the size and the universality of the genre, and the difficulties of locating or viewing more than a tiny fraction of them, generalizations about the biofilm must be tentative. Yet years of tracking such works suggest to me that the biofilm can be seen in terms of four (admittedly) baggy and arbitrary categories: the biopic of Hollywood's studio era; the "serious" biofilm that has for a long time been made in Europe and other parts of the world, and has more recently come to Hollywood; the documentary biography; and the innovative or experimental bio, which presents a life in the form of a fragmented or a chronological drama rather than a traditional linear story.

In each of these categories, significant works have been created—films that provide knowledge of, insight into, and interpretation of the lives of individuals; films that let us see, hear, and understand a great deal about not only the person but, in many cases, his or her historical milieu. In each category, we can find works that fulfill Nadel's definition of biography as "fundamentally a narrative which has as its primary task the enactment of character and place through language. . . ."[13] A major difference here is that the word "language" must be made to include the words "image," "color," and "sound." Those additions, along with the changes that occur when biography is transformed from a literary narrative into a dramatic production, ensure that the biofilm will always deliver a rather different figure from what we get in a written biography. This difference means that such films may not only be seen as a new sort of biography, but one that at its best can also serve to highlight the shortcomings of the written form.

The contribution of the biofilm, at least to historians, may seem most obvious in the second category, what I have labeled "the serious biofilm." By this I mean films in which the director has either worked closely with a historical consultant and/or adhered faithfully to events as recounted in one or more written biographies, and in doing so has indulged in a minimal amount of invention with regard to characters and events. Into this category we could place such a film as Julie Taymor's *Frida*, which tells of the life, loves, and art of Mexican painter Frida Kahlo. The film has not been free of criticism, but this has to do more with the film's emphasis than with invention. Objections have been made to the way Kahlo's activities as a committed member of the Mexican Communist Party, as well as a painter of her own tortured body and soul, have been downplayed. Countering such a critique is not difficult. Since Kahlo is known primarily for her paintings (which have much personal but little social content) as well as her relationship with Diego Rivera, the downplaying of her political beliefs, however fervently held, is only part of a strategy to highlight her real contribution to the world of art. This response is not meant to put an end to criticism but to illustrate that at least this biofilm (and, obviously, others) can be debated for its overall portrait in much the same way as one would debate any traditional biography—less over the accuracy of individual bits of data than over the whole interpretation.

More surprising than the claim that such "serious" biofilms present plausible portraits of their subjects may be the assertion that even in the standard Hollywood biopic, it is possible to find an important interpretation of a life—and even suggestions about a different sort of biographical thinking. Drawing on the scholarship of J. E. Smyth, I wish to make such an argument for director John Ford's *Young Mr. Lincoln*. This 1939 film was hailed on its release by well-known critic and early film historian Terry Ramsaye as a unique biographical work that went beyond a mere recording of historical events. But such enthusiasm for the film as biography has not been shared by later scholars—least of all, historians. Lincoln experts see it as "a historical travesty and folksy perversion." Mark Reinhart, author of a book about Lincoln on-screen, writes, "It is unfortunate that Young Mr. Lincoln has come to be regarded by many as one of the greatest portrayals of all time, because the film's script and Henry Fonda's performance do not accurately reflect the Lincoln of History." [14]

The problem for such critics is twofold: first, Ford's film is full of invented or imagined situations (Lincoln standing down a lynch mob or settling a case between two clients by threatening to bang their heads together), and second, it completely distorts chronology by bringing together events that happened years apart. Most egregiously, the film moves Lincoln's famous legal victory, the 1858 William "Duff" Armstrong murder trial, back to a much earlier point in his career. And while it keeps the dramatic climax of the trial, the one in which Lincoln famously uses

ROBERT ROSENSTONE

an almanac on the phases of the moon to show that it was too dark for a witness to have seen what he claimed to have seen, the film drastically alters many of the specific events and circumstances of that trial. *Young Mr. Lincoln* is not, however, a complete invention. Nor does it wholly ignore data. The dramatic opening scene shows the young attorney making his first electoral speech in 1832, in the precise words recorded by his law partner, William Herndon: "My politics are short and sweet, like the old woman's dance." But it's not the words that create the character. The body language of Henry Fonda as the lanky frontiersman, slouching on the porch railing of a store before his talk, moving awkwardly into position in front of the small crowd, fiddling with his hands, and speaking in a high, midwestern drawl—all these elements perfectly exemplify how film creates a kind of dimensional, almost tactile historical figure in a way that is beyond the capabilities of the written word. Here a skilled performer takes what we know from historical accounts (that Lincoln started out as an awkward country rube and never fully shed those characteristics) and embodies that knowledge into movements and moments that allow the audience to feel as if they are (apparently) witnessing the past.

More provocative as portraits and perhaps more suggestive in terms of the possibilities of biography are those works that can be placed at one end of the spectrum—innovative or experimental biofilms. Elsewhere I have devoted an entire essay to one of these, *Walker,* directed by Alex Cox, a portrait of the monomaniacal American buccaneer who invaded Nicaragua with a small army in the 1850s, stayed on to become that country's president, and upon being pushed out by armies from other Central American countries, burned the capital city of Granada to the ground. Cast as a kind of black and absurdist comedy, and full of overt anachronisms (Mercedes automobiles, *Time* magazine, and computer terminals in the 1850s), the film nonetheless both absorbs and comments upon a long tradition of representing the man and his adventures. Equally suggestive is *Thirty-two Short Films about Glenn Gould,* a portrait of the great Canadian pianist cast in the form of his most famous recording, Johann Sebastian Bach's *The Goldberg Variations.*

To explore the potential and reach of the biofilm, I want to examine three dramatic features about the life of a single figure, John Reed, the American poet, journalist, and revolutionary whose book, *Ten Days That Shook the World,* is the classic account of the Bolshevik Revolution. That these works—*Reed: Insurgent Mexico* (1973), by Mexican director Paul Leduc; *Red Bells* (1982), by Soviet director Sergei Bondarchuk; and *Reds* (1981), by American director Warren Beatty—are the products of

Warren Beatty as John Reed, Reds *(Paramount, 1981; courtesy Photofest)*

different film traditions and filmmakers with clearly different ideologies will help to suggest something about the range and possibilities of the genre. (In the interest of full disclosure, I must explain that I both wrote a biography of Reed—*Romantic Revolutionary: A Biography of John Reed* [1975]—and served for eight years as historical consultant in both the preproduction and the filming stages of *Reds.*) [15]

These three biofilms may be devoted to the same subject, but they are quite different in their approach and aesthetic qualities, as well as in the period of the life that they cover. One thing they do share is a similar theme, a theme that also tends to drive biographical books devoted to Reed—the desire to explain how and why this privileged young man from a wealthy Portland, Oregon, family, a Harvard graduate who in his twenties became one of the highest paid reporters in the United States, ended up not just writing about two revolutions (those in Mexico and Russia) but ultimately embracing the Bolsheviks, helping to organize the Communist Labor Party of the United States, going as a delegate to the Second Congress of the Communist International in Moscow in 1920, and then attending the Congress of the People of the East in Baku, where he contracted the typhus that led to his death. Reed's body lay in state as a hero of the revolution before it was buried alongside other Russian notables in the embankment in front of the Kremlin wall.

My own book on Reed carries him from cradle to grave in some 400 pages, which gives ample space to elaborate on everything from family antecedents (his maternal grandfather was one of the richest pioneers in

ROBERT ROSENSTONE

Oregon), to early psychological development (he was a sickly child who had to struggle to overcome some early physical handicaps and fears), to the multiple contexts in which he lived—the social movements of his childhood (his father was a militant Progressive who exposed corruption in the Oregon timber industry); the battles for political and educational reform at twentieth-century Harvard (he was active as a journalist and member of the Socialist Club and various international societies); the artistic and sexual ferment of Greenwich Village in the teens (where modernism in the arts, personal liberation, sexual experimentation, and political radicalism were the norm); the desert and mountains of northern Mexico where he rode as a correspondent with the troops of Pancho Villa (he sympathized with the peons exploited by large landowners); the trenches on both the western and eastern fronts during the early years of the First World War (as he saw it, a senseless slaughter for no purpose other than to benefit capitalism); and the excitement of Petrograd during what he would label the great Ten Days (which seemed a culmination of the radicalism espoused in Greenwich Village). If the filmmakers do not have the luxury of detailing all these phenomena as a way of explaining Reed's movement toward revolution, they are able to evoke many of them.

Unlike written biographies, few biofilms attempt to cover the entire span of a life. To this general rule, the Reed films are no exception. The one with the narrowest time frame, the one hour and forty-five minute *Reed: Insurgent Mexico*, deals with no more than half of the four-month period the young journalist spent in Mexico, largely focusing on his weeks with the horseback troops of General Tomas Urbina and his time with Pancho Villa before and during his army's advance on the strategic city of Torreón. *Red Bells* (1982) consists of two two-hour films—the first devoted to Reed in Mexico and the second to his weeks in Petrograd before and during the Bolshevik Revolution. Unlike *Insurgent Mexico*, each of these two films encompasses Reed's relationship with a woman—in the first, his wealthy lover, Mabel Dodge; in the second, his wife, Louise Bryant. *Reds* (1981), save for a one-shot opening sequence, begins after his Mexican adventures and takes three hours and fifteen minutes to follow Reed from his first meeting with Louise Bryant in Portland in 1915 to his death in Moscow in the fall of 1920. Unlike the others, this film devotes a great deal of time to his personal life, focusing on his relationship with Bryant, as well as the milieus in which he flourished—the radical subculture of Greenwich Village in the teens, the socialist sects out of which the Communist Labor Party grew, and the revolutionary environment of Petrograd and Moscow.

John Reed (Beatty) and Louise Bryant (Diane Keaton). From Reds *(Paramount, 1981; courtesy Photofest)*

Left to right: Eugene O'Neill (Jack Nicholson), Bryant (Keaton), and Reed (Beatty). From Reds *(Paramount, 1981; courtesy Photofest)*

Insurgent Mexico, shot in sepia tone no doubt to emulate the photos of the early twentieth century, stresses the personal over the public life. Reed is the focus of attention in every sequence, and though the visual and verbal languages (point of view shots, cutaways, conversations) resonate with larger issues of exploitation, justice, and revolution, the camera always returns to events Reed saw and experienced. A good deal of the film, based on Reed's autobiography, focuses on his time with La Tropa, General Urbina's cavalry. The book can be read as a coming-of-age story, a tale of a naive young American achieving manhood and political insight through his companionship both with La Tropa and his encounters with Villa—and what is subtext on Reed's pages becomes the organizing theme of the film. At first the young man seems to be a cool, collected sort who when asked by soldiers why he doesn't carry a gun, makes the argument that words are as important as deeds. That these attitudes are something of a facade becomes clear when, in the midst of a fiesta, a drunken Reed confesses his fears to a comrade—he is not the man his father was, a true battler who died in his struggles against corrupt power. He is a dreamer, someone who never goes all the way, who is afraid to plunge fully into the fray, who remains a reporter because, even though he loves the revolutionary cause, he fears death on the battlefield.

Later Reed begins to wonder if conveying the facts is enough. When one sees injustice, isn't it necessary to act? Reed comes close to doing just that during an evening assault, but as he prepares to toss a primitive grenade, Pancho Villa shows up on horseback and takes it away from him, shouting, "You're a journalist, not a soldier. I need journalists more than soldiers!" The next day when Reed walks through the streets of a liberated town, as the victorious troops ride by, yelling and firing their guns in the air, he takes off his jacket, wraps it around his right hand, and smashes the plate glass window of a store—and the frame freezes, ending the film, save for a voice-over that links Mexico to his later time in Russia. This final action, if gratuitous, is not taken from the book. Rather, it is the director's attempt to create a visual metaphor that expresses Reed's commitment and foreshadows future actions that would not transfer easily to the screen within this narrative—his passionate articles in favor of the Mexican Revolution; the interview with President Woodrow Wilson in which he urged military backing for Villa; the writing of *Insurgent Mexico* itself, which turned Villa into a hero and Reed into one of the most highly visible journalists in the country; and finally, his involvement as a partisan in the Bolshevik Revolution.

Red Bells lies at the far end of the biofilm spectrum from *Insurgent Mexico*—in scope, style, and vision. The two-hour segment dealing with

Mexico is an epic, a spectacle in color and wide-screen in which our hero disappears from sight for long periods of time while we watch thousands of horseback and foot soldiers engage in bloody military actions across vast, desert landscapes, attack huge haciendas, or battle their way through the narrow streets of adobe villages.

Unlike the more intimate Mexican film, *Red Bells I* provides a series of flashbacks to earlier events in Reed's life. A couple of sequences suggest his growing political consciousness. But the majority of them provide visions of the world of glamour, celebrity, and ease that he left behind. At the center of that world is Mabel Dodge, the wealthy hostess of a Manhattan salon who, after becoming Reed's lover, whisks him off to her villa near Florence, where leisure activities are the order of the day—lively fiestas in nearby villages, piano recitals in the villa's elegant public rooms, or lovemaking with Dodge in her sumptuous bedroom. She represents a world in which Art is the highest value, and so she keeps trying to make Reed forget the world of social concerns, abandon journalism, and return to his earlier forms of creative writing—"you are a poet," she says over and over. "This is a marvelous place to forget the world and write poetry."

The film relates many of the same events as does *Insurgent Mexico* (but depicts them far more lavishly). The choice Reed faces in *Red Bells I* does not (at least overtly) involve fears of death, as in *Insurgent Mexico*. Here it's a tug between two sorts of life, the lavish but effete lifestyle of Dodge and the more rugged life of front line journalism—a life that also suggests commitment to the downtrodden of the world. We see a nervous Reed in the trenches at Torreón who overcomes his fear, charges up a hill into gunfire alongside Villa's troops, and stops to toss a hand grenade at the enemy. His joy in the explosion indicates that he has made his commitment.

Red Bells II has the same epic qualities as the first, only here the mass movements involve sailors, soldiers, and factory workers who play out their revolutionary drama on the wide stage of Petrograd, with its broad boulevards, huge squares, and lavish palaces, its churches, fortresses, canals, and bridges that span the wide Neva River. Once again Reed disappears for long stretches of time as we watch the revolutionary events unfold.

Most of the incidents are taken directly from the pages of *Ten Days That Shook the World*, but the accomplishment of *Red Bells II* lies less in its dramatic story than in its filmic qualities of movement, production design, and montage. Events are shot in the original settings, adding authenticity. One extended sequence, enormously evocative of the clashes

ROBERT ROSENSTONE

and contradictions of the revolutionary situation, cuts back and forth between a ballet at the elegant Marinsky Theater—with Bryant and Reed, wearing formal dress, in attendance—and the restless streets of the city, with Reed always on the move through the crowds, asking questions, listening to debates, talking to workers, eavesdropping on conversations, watching the newly formed Red Guards drill, trying unsuccessfully to find out what groups have ordered particular roadblocks in front of the Kazan Cathedral—the Provisional Government, the Soviets, the military? Nobody seems to know.

The climax for Reed, the Bolsheviks, and the film is the taking of the Winter Palace. Unlike the sequence in Sergei Eisenstein's well-known film *October,* this one does not depict a huge battle but something more like the token resistance that historians record. Reed and Bryant are there—as they were historically. Twice, earlier in the film, she has turned to him and asked, "Are you now a Bolshevik?" Each time he has slightly equivocated, saying words to the effect of "I like what they're doing," or "I'm beginning to think so." In the final sequence, as he starts to follow the troops toward the Winter Palace, she asks him again. This time his answer is clear: "I'm with them." A minute later, as he watches Red Guards climb a barricade before the palace door, he stops, raises his fist in the air, and shouts: "Hooray. Hooray. Hooray."

Compared to a traditional written biography that follows a subject from birth to death (such as my own work on Reed), *Reds* focuses on a short period in the life of its subject. Compared to the other films discussed here, it covers a rather large portion of Reed's life—not a period of weeks but the last five of his thirty-three years. Its geographical canvas is also broad, with American sequences in Portland, New York City, and Provincetown, and foreign ones in France, Finland, Petrograd, Moscow, and Baku. If *Insurgent Mexico* may be seen as a coming-of-age tale, and the two chapters of *Red Bells* as epics in which the individual is less important than great events, *Reds* is a love story or domestic drama in which almost as much screen time is devoted to Louise Bryant as to Jack Reed.

The first half of the film intertwines their stormy relationship and subsequent marriage with the political events that draw Reed, first as a reporter and then, increasingly, as a participant. Bryant leaves her husband and follows Reed to New York, and her introduction to the cultural and political avant-garde of Greenwich Village becomes our own. In one extended sequence, the poles of the world they inhabit are brilliantly juxtaposed as the film cuts back and forth between close, crowded shots of Reed and Bryant dancing at the Liberal Club—the different steps they

Reed (Beatty) and Bryant (Keaton). From Reds *(Paramount, 1981; courtesy Photofest)*

attempt and the different, seasonal costumes marking the passage of time—and close, crowded shots of the two of them, with friends, lounging in bars or sitting in Reed's living room, arguing over social theory and politics, tossing around names like Marx, Engels, Freud, Jung, and Debs. There is little real explication of ideas here—just enough of a gesture to indicate that radical notions are very much part of this subculture.

They arrive in Russia during the volatile month of September 1917, as the country teeters on the brink of revolution. The shift from reporter to activist takes place on the day the couple enters a factory in which the workers are heatedly debating whether or not to support the Bolsheviks. Called to the platform to speak on behalf of the American workers, he shouts that they are waiting for the Russians to lead them toward world revolution. Amid thunderous cheers, he tries to get back to Bryant, who is still in the audience, but he is mobbed and the crowd comes between them—as the revolution will for the rest of their lives. Their gaze across the shoulders of working men leads into a montage in which scenes of the Bolshevik takeover (troops marching, seizing key points in Petrograd, entering the Winter Palace) are intercut with silhouetted images of Reed and Bryant making love—and all of these are bridged by a powerful chorus singing *The Internationale.* The metaphor is clear (if a bit

ROBERT ROSENSTONE

Max Eastman (Edward Hermann), Reed (Beatty), and Bryant (Keaton). From Reds *(Paramount, 1981; courtesy Photofest)*

strange)—the uniting of the couple and the uniting of the Russian proletariat in the revolution are both acts of love.

Of all the John Reed biofilms, *Reds* is the one that indulges most frequently in such fictive moves as condensation, alteration, and outright invention.[16] With a few minor exceptions, the others are content to take characters and incidents directly from Reed's own books, though none of them questions to what extent those works were the product of the writer's own inventiveness. All the films also draw to some extent on other historical sources—this is equally true of the major sections in *Red Bells I* devoted to Zapata's war and to the intimate scene in *Insurgent Mexico* when Reed confesses to his lifelong weaknesses, doubts, and fears. Since such a moment does not occur in his own book, it has to be based on a larger reading of his life—as well as on the nature of the medium and the dramatic form. One can read the coming-of-age story of *Insurgent Mexico* as an extended personal confession—so what the director has done is to translate that confession into a dramatized moment on-screen.

If the other films stick more closely to written texts and to verifiable historical fact, it may be because their time span is short and their geographic reach not very broad. *Reds* not only covers the events of five years but takes upon itself the task of depicting multiple social worlds and political movements. Some of its factual errors are flagrant: Reed

Bryant (Keaton) awaits John Reed's return. Reds *(Paramount, 1981; courtesy Photofest)*

and Bryant riding a train from France to Petrograd in 1917 without encountering German armies. Others involve the kinds of condensations and displacements one finds in every historical film. Take the opening sequence, in which a nude photo of Bryant causes a scandal at a Portland art exhibition. This invention instantly shows that she was a highly unconventional woman—and can be linked historically to a series of photos of herself naked on a beach that she sent to Reed the following year. Or take the subsequent sequence, Reed's speech to the Liberal Club. Asked by the man who introduces him to answer the question "what is this war about?" he answers with a single word: "Profits." In truth, Reed spoke to the club about the war not in 1915 but the year before, and he spoke at length. But that one word brilliantly encapsulates the message of his earlier speech and, indeed, everything else he had written for the previous two years about a conflict that he called, in the title of his first article on the topic, "A Trader's War."

In the introduction to *Ten Days That Shook the World,* John Reed calls his book "a slice of intensified history." [17] On the following pages he successfully captures the confused, even chaotic feeling of Petrograd in the crucial days of revolution, as he cuts from one site to another, breaking an already jumpy narrative with the texts of speeches, newspaper articles, and the contents of posters. Doing so, he was helping to invent a new kind of journalism, termed by one scholar "a narrative immediacy . . . that makes the reader a vicarious participant in the historic event."[18] He was also anticipating to some extent the way films would create historical—and biographical—worlds. If the biofilm can never achieve the richness of detail or depth of analysis of a long, written biography, it can, as we see in the examples above, give the viewer a slice of a life, intensified by the genre of drama and the power of the medium. It may not be able to provide deep psychological insight or extensive descriptions of particular intellectual or political milieus, but it can suggest with a terrifying immediacy how the past looked and how people moved, felt, spoke, and acted—in time. Unlike the written word, the biofilm, even in its flashbacks, always functions in the present tense, suggesting, even making you feel as if you have lived through those moments of experience.

Like history, what you take away from a biofilm depends upon what you bring to it. My readings of these three Reed films are obviously informed by the years of study a specialist devotes to a topic. How they would have been read by their target audiences is difficult to discern, as is the question of how they would be understood by audiences in those same countries today.

What I am suggesting is that biofilms, like all works that deal with the past, are entities with unstable meanings that shift over the years, that they are read and understood according to specific viewing audiences or individuals. Less than full-blown portraits, they should be seen and understood as slices of lives, interventions into particular discourses, extended metaphors meant to suggest more than their limited time frames can convey. Each of the films about Reed certainly engages the traces of his life one can find in research collections, as well as the figure portrayed in history books. As do all biographies, the films reconfigure him, comment upon the other works, enter into the debates over his life, and revivify some of its moments in an effort to make him meaningful to a new audience.

None of the Reeds presented on-screen is quite the same one that I created in *Romantic Revolutionary* in 1975, nor is any of them the one created by Granville Hicks in 1936 or Eric Homberger in 1990.[19] Yet each in its own way certainly fulfills Nadel's definition of biography as "fundamentally a narrative which has as its primary task the enactment of character and place through language," though the language here is visual, aural, and dramatic. The Reeds in these works are presented at different times of life and through a different aesthetic, but they can be seen as recognizably built on the same historical figure—the ambitious writer and reporter who became first a chronicler and then a partisan of revolution. If the strategies in the works differ, an argument can certainly be made in favor of each as a genuine biographical form—the intimate, psychological portrait of a fearful man who grows to radical commitment by his encounter with the Mexican Revolution; the person whose individuality is less important than his symbolic or emblematic role, a figure less remembered for his individual predilections and tastes and more for the larger historical events he witnessed and chronicled; and the man torn between love and activism, who spends much of his life trying to balance the demands of the personal and those of the political, the private world of love and the public world of social change. All of these riff off the same set of historical and biographical data used by all biographers of Reed, and all are valid ways of making meaning out of his life and carrying that meaning to a new generation. None could be called definitive, but then again no biographical interpretation ever is. Each of these films, if we learn how to read it, has much to tell us about the man and his personal struggles, and each suggests something about the larger issues of the times in which he lived. What more can one ask of a biofilm—or, for that matter, of a biography?

NOTES

1. Ronald Bergan, "What Ever Happened to the Biopic," *Films and Filming* 346 (July 1983): 22.

2. George F. Custen, *Bio/Pics: How Hollywood Constructed Public History* (New Brunswick, NJ: Rutgers University Press, 1992), 7.

3. George F. Custen, "The Mechanical Life in the Age of Human Reproduction: American Biopics, 1961–1980," *Biography* 23, no. 1 (Winter 2000): 127–59.

4. Custen, *Bio/Pics*, 4–5.

5. Ibid.

6. Roland Barthes, unknown.

7. Carolyn G. Heilbrun, "Is Biography Fiction?" *Soundings: An Interdisciplinary Journal* 86, no. 2–3 (Summer/Fall 1993): 297.

8. Paula R. Backscheider, *Reflections on Biography* (New York: Oxford University Press, 2000), 18.

9. Ira Nadel, *Biography: Fiction, Fact, and Form* (New York: St. Martin's Press, 1984), 6.

10. Hayden White, *Tropics of Discourse: Essays in Cultural Criticism* (Baltimore: Johns Hopkins University Press, 1978), 99.

11. Quoted in George Lukacs, *The Historical Novel* (Lincoln: University of Nebraska Press, 1983), 62.

12. "Inventing Historical Truth on the Silver Screen," *Cineaste* 29, no. 2 (Spring 2004): 29–33.

13. Nadel, *Biography*, 8.

ROBERT ROSENSTONE

14. J. E. Smyth, "Young Mr. Lincoln: Between Myth and History in 1939," *Rethinking History: The Journal of Theory and Practice* 7 (Summer 2003): 193–214, quotation on 194.

15. *Romantic Revolutionary: A Biography of John Reed* (New York: Alfred A. Knopf, 1975; New York: Vintage, 1981; Cambridge, MA: Harvard University Press, 1992).

16. See my essay "The Historical Film: Looking at the Past in a Post Literate Age," in *Visions of the Past* (Cambridge, MA: Harvard University Press, 1995), especially 71–75.

17. John Reed, *Ten Days That Shook the World* (New York: International, 1934), xxxiii.

18. Daniel W. Lehman, *John Reed and the Writing of Revolution* (Athens: Ohio University Press, 2002), 190.

19. Granville Hicks, *John Reed: The Making of a Revolutionary* (New York: Macmillan, 1936); Eric Homberger, *John Reed* (Manchester, UK: Manchester University Press, 1990).

HISTORY IS WHAT REMAINS
CINEMA'S CHALLENGE TO
IDEAS ABOUT THE PAST

....

GEOFF PINGREE

Although it relies solely on documented biographical and auto-biographical sources, Jay Rosenblatt's *Human Remains* (1998)[1] recounts a most unexpected history. The film deploys its archival materials to render strange five otherwise renowned protagonists: Hitler, Mussolini, Stalin, Franco, and Mao. Well known to audiences for kindred legacies of violent, totalitarian rule, these dictators appear in Rosenblatt's movie in terms of little-known, often repellent, intimate traits.

The film's focus on the quotidian peculiarities of historical monsters is intriguing in its own right, but this strategy does more by framing the despots' relations with the media in provocative ways. These figures are notorious for using expansive propaganda machinery to consolidate and exercise political power, in part by attempting to mold unassailable public images of themselves. By weaving together a catalog of base personal anomalies with seldom seen actuality footage, *Human Remains* overtly transforms these infamous icons into banal eccentrics, thereby defusing the tyrants' self-fashioned historical aura.[2]

Consequently, and perhaps more importantly, the movie implicitly challenges the underlying relations among truth, history, and media. *Human Remains*, itself a media artifact, embodies a cinematic mode of narration[3] that questions the very role of media (including so-called historical media) in the formation of icons and auras; it is a motion picture that reflects creatively on history's own processes of mediation.

As these abstract claims about a film barely thirty minutes long may seem ambitious, they beg further discussion. To initiate that discussion,

I begin with the tangible—a brief description of how the movie looks and sounds to a viewer, because *Human Remains* owes much of its power to the *experience* of seeing and hearing it, such that the film's emotional impact precedes any of its rational implications.

Sound arrives first: a congested train whistle blares, metal brakes screech. Immediately a locomotive appears, enshrouded in clouds of smoke, moving forward in slow motion along its tracks, passing an engine moving in the opposite direction; "LOCOMOTION FILMS presents," the first title, becomes visible. Then a moment of silence, and the screen fades to black. A softened, two-note kettledrum beat initiates the picture's haunting musical score. The beat rises and then merges with a gloomy, bass string and muted woodwind composition that climbs the scale and falls, climbs and falls. A medium close-up, point-of-view shot (also in slow motion, within a canted frame) accompanies this somber aural theme. It provides something like what the steam engine's own perspective might be, were it gazing down over the rails that—first inexplicably crisscrossing, then becoming steadily parallel—pass beneath it.

The screen fades to black again, though the dismal audio theme continues, swelling portentously. A grainy, black-and-white image appears, portraying in medium close-up the profile of a dark-haired man, dressed in a suit, holding on his knee a smiling little girl. The footage (like all before it, in slow motion) is oddly disconcerting, as the girl reaches her hand inside the man's suit jacket, then removes it, repeatedly, mechanically; the footage is being looped, replayed. The sound composition deepens as it unexpectedly drops in key, augmenting the feeling of threat. Onscreen, the man turns toward the camera and is suddenly familiar: Adolf Hitler pulls the little girl a bit closer, displaying a faint, almost mischievous smile.

An audible "poof!" and the faint crackle of fire mix with the disquieting music, and the image of Hitler and his young companion begins to melt into yellowish, asymmetrical spots, the celluloid itself apparently snagging and burning inside the projector. Yet the musical theme persists, reaching a fearful climax, and as the screen fills with a swirl of gray smoke and black ash—dotted momentarily by what look like two bright, full moons—the film's title appears, superimposed in bright red letters. The movie's illusive disposition now evident, the screen fades to black, and there descends a silence broken only by the whisper of a desolate wind.

The grating, metallic sound of digging introduces a lone human figure, shrouded in darkness, thrusting a shovel into charcoal gray, dusty matter, in an equally charcoal gray, dusty place. Is this figure excavating a grave? Is this place a cemetery? The ever-digging shoveler will materialize time and again, heralding the appearance on-screen of each new dictator, but for now, the figure's vaguely unnatural movements indicate more play in the movie's speed of motion. The screen fades to black anew, and a new audio tone, the most menacing yet—a low string, heavy and brooding—emerges to hover uneasily over the film.

In close-up, Hitler appears again, though now in a disorienting negative freeze-frame. Motion resumes as he leans back in a chair, then forward. Suddenly Hitler is transformed into an easily recognizable positive image: his eerily white hair, mustache, suit, and tie turn their usual black; his unnaturally black face and collared shirt bleach to their familiar white. Hitler leans back again, rests his head, gazes contemplatively offscreen, and the soundtrack's first human sound—a tired, desolate sigh, striking in its subtlety—initiates the movie's voice-over narration.

Presumably the source of the melancholy utterance, Hitler starts to speak, beginning the first of five confessional chapters. Each tyrant has his own deviant secrets to tell, and this establishes the first-person, retrospective point of view that will govern the film. "I was an artist and had wished to retire from politics altogether," he wearily recalls, adding, almost contemptuously, "the only things that endure are the works of human genius!" Affirming his love of movies, he exclaims, "And of course I loved the ones that Leni [Riefenstahl] made." As he pauses, a medium shot of his smirking face abruptly becomes an extreme close-up of his (smirking) mustached mouth, and he adds, ominously, "By the way . . . we were *very* close."

Setting a pattern that his fellow dictators will follow, the führer proceeds to comment cryptically on a bizarre range of matters, mostly personal. He endured stomach cramps and eczema; he was a lax vegetarian who knew that his beloved noodle soup was made with chicken stock and that his favorite dumplings contained liver; he had a weakness for chocolate éclairs; he suffered from flatulence; he eschewed coffee in favor of mineral water and chamomile tea (which he also used as an enema); and he had just one testicle. Though he enjoyed multiple romantic affairs, Hitler loved only one woman—his niece—but he locked her in his apartment and took a trip to Hamburg, only to return and find her dead, a suicide. The Nazi leader required his bed quilt folded according to a precise design; he saw no beauty in nature; he relished pornography; and he had his dog, Blondie, destroyed the day before he died.

As Hitler concludes his odd testimony, the film's emotional tone becomes more elusive and increasingly complex. His pronouncements, and the images they accompany, share an uneven relationship—at times one

Adolf Hitler, from Human Remains *(Jay Rosenblatt, 1998)*

illustrates the other; other times no logical connection is discernible. They are intermittently funny, repellent, mysterious, and sobering; their association is sufficiently convoluted and random to inhibit spectators' confidence about the appropriateness of their reactions.

The shoveler, speechless yet evocative—a Greek chorus of one, a Shakespearean fool—appears once again, still digging, although now it is difficult to say whether this figure is excavating or covering something up. The pattern is set: Mussolini will soon turn up, followed by the shoveler, then Stalin, the shoveler, Franco, the shoveler, Mao, and finally the shoveler again. As Mussolini shows off by playing with a lion cub or sledding bare-chested down a snowy mountain; as a sneering Stalin condemns his favorite daughter for sleeping with Jews; as a pious and falsely modest Franco casts his fishing rod or shoots partridges; as Mao brags of never brushing his teeth and of washing his genitals in the bodies of his women—we can't help but ask: What kind of film is this? What kind of history?

Not long ago, I delivered a lecture on Spain, its civil war, and the role that documentary film played in that conflict. Afterward, my eminent respondent, Cary Nelson, suggested that "there are no decisive Spanish facts."[4] His provocative claim was meant to suggest that studying the Spanish Civil War, even now, more than six decades after its conclusion, is bound to be "indecisive," since such an inquiry requires one to pass through a maze of powerful and divided narratives. That war's clash of politics and culture left a legacy of uncertain and contested meaning that continues still (certainly in Spain), as many of the issues and questions the conflict has symbolized remain unsettled.[5]

Hence Nelson's belief that most writing about the Spanish Civil War does little more than confirm the profound, disorienting complexity of the conflict and representations by which we know it. When in *Human Remains* Rosenblatt depicts Franco, he is depicting a man who, entangled inextricably within a dialectic of his own self-serving propaganda and of that which opposed him, was both crusader and usurper, savior and destroyer. This anecdote underscores the crucial difference between the complexity of an event and the complexity of a representation of that event. Though innately related, each has an independent existence, as it were, with different, potentially conflicting, implications and consequences.

In the course of my research on the Spanish War, I often have wondered if the histories of that conflict—entrenched as they are in the oppositional rhetoric that characterized the war itself—cannot help but also be histories of history itself. Nelson's words seemed to echo George Orwell's famous comment—made about the war in Spain after he had participated in and tried to write about it—that "history stopped in 1936." For Orwell, the war in Spain foreclosed a conception of history as "a considerable body of fact which would have been agreed to by almost everyone," a conception in which the facts were "more or less discoverable." Although Orwell had already learned to distrust historical bias and inaccuracy, the Civil War taught him to fear that "the very concept of objective truth [was] fading out of the world." He later noted that in Spain he observed for the first time "newspaper reports which did not bear any relation to the facts, not even the relationship which is implied in an ordinary lie." And thus he lamented, "What is peculiar to our own age is the abandonment of the idea that history *could* be truthfully written."[6]

Orwell was not declaring, with Fukuyama-like momentousness, the end of History.[7] Rather, he was mourning the loss of a particular set of shared understandings, what Kenneth Burke might call "attitudes toward history,"[8] the loss of a certain perspective on the relationship between the events of the real world and our ability to continuously account for those events through narrative. Lost, in Orwell's view, was not the actual possibility of a totally objective history—he had always presumed the quixotic folly in that—but rather a process of fashioning history that, through its regard for the *ideal* of objectivity, would allow for a coherent diversity of meaningful, if imperfect and biased, perspectives. What Orwell saw endangered in the Spanish Civil War was the notion of history as pluralistic dialogue, as struggle for consensus.[9]

We can infer this concern through Orwell's accounts of his experience in Spain, which consistently endorse an implicit alternative to both a traditional ideal of history as unbending—fixed and objective—and to a political use of history as something almost wholly subjective and manipulable. In Orwell's view, neither approach conceives of our relationship with the past as a tension between the wish for neutral vision and an acceptance, however reluctant, that such vision is not possible. While we can imagine accounts of the past that are perfectly accurate—God's-eye views, we might say—we are capable of composing only contingent ones.[10]

I believe Orwell's wisdom lies in his suggestion that a useful rendering of the past is an admittedly imperfect construction that nonetheless gains substance through an honest and fluid pursuit of accuracy. Such an *ideal-regarding* history is not pure relativism, does not accept that "anything goes," but rather is principled in its pursuit of historical understanding.[11] Indeed, it acknowledges that the *wish* for an unobstructed, empirical view of the past is a *creative* impulse necessary for any depiction—for any constructive imagining—of what has gone before.[12]

In Orwell's view, then (or at least in my reading of it), to assess meaningfully the quality of a historical account, one must not only evaluate that account's factual accuracy, but must also recognize—and reflect upon—its nature *as an account* in the first place. This approach may seem like old news, a notion accepted, expressly or otherwise, by most historians. But it is practiced less often, and less reliably, than it is embraced publicly. To speak of the difficulty of addressing an unmasterable past is not the same as to confront that past with an active awareness that the struggle to know is, indeed, a struggle that never ends.

Cinema, which began with grand aspirations for facilitating an objective view of the past, can play a unique and vital role in this struggle. Early film theorists often spoke of the medium with a confidence—or fear—that has typically accompanied powerful new technologies.[13] Indeed, many early practitioners were exuberant about film's potential. The influential American director and producer D. W. Griffith, for example, claimed in 1915 that the "time will come, and in less than ten years, when the children in the public schools will be taught practically everything by moving pictures. Certainly they will never be obliged to read history again." Griffith imagined a future in which history would exist reliably as a film archive that afforded a comprehensive visual record of the past:

> There will be long rows of boxes or pillars . . . classified and indexed. . . . At each box a push button and before each box a seat. Suppose you wish to 'read up' on a certain episode in Napoleon's life.

GEOFF PINGREE

Instead of consulting all the authorities, wading laboriously through a host of books, and ending bewildered, without a clear idea of exactly what did happen and confused . . . by conflicting opinions about what did happen, you will merely seat yourself at a . . . window, in a scientifically prepared room, press the button, and actually see what happened.

There will be no opinions expressed. You will merely be present at the making of history. All the work of writing, revising, collating, and reproducing will have been carefully attended to by a corps of recognized experts, and you will have received a vivid and complete expression.[14]

Griffith's utopian perspective aside, cinema was, relative to other forms of visual representation, exceedingly serious about capturing the past and committed to apprehending a scientific impression of reality through nonhuman and thus infallible means, with better-than-human precision.[15] In this respect, cinema replicated many of the ideals of history itself.

Despite the ceaseless march forward of film technology, these idealistic early visions were tempered by the medium's inevitable material restrictions, which forced cinema to deal explicitly with problems of representation—including problems of historical representation.[16] Film's physical limits, in fact, help make sense of current ongoing debates about the relationship between history and the movies, controversies that seem to ignite anew with each film (*JFK*, for example, or *Schindler's List*) that treats a disputed set of consequential events. That *things happened*, that *events occurred*—on these premises we can all agree. But the difficulty lies in *how* we negotiate the inevitable distance between us and these events and happenings. In assessing the particular history that a film depicts, it is at least as important to think carefully about the mechanisms and rules according to which that depiction has been shaped as it is to debate the depiction's meaning. This exercise proceeds, after all, from a position of immense presumed authority, a state of mind that assumes an unmediated, ex post facto understanding of the events a film portrays.[17]

Curiously, documentary has been relatively overlooked in discussions of film and history. Yet this mode seems central to questions about how we represent the past, if only because it shares with history a sober view of its own commitment to a dispassionate portrayal of the past. It is as if the debates surrounding film and history have looked beyond documentary because the mode's seriousness of purpose and accuracy of depiction are already settled questions. But of course that is not the case. Implicitly positioning dramatic or fiction film against documentary in this way yields too narrow—too binary—a calculus, too categorical a map for understanding the broad, multidimensional relationship between the process of representation and a past that is, in essential ways, unreachable, except by representation.

It is not a surprise that the rivalry between film and history to speak for the past emerged primarily around discussions of fiction films. Movie producers, directors, writers, or studios that have reworked existing historical materials typically have been seen by traditional and serious historians as provocateurs who seem to say, "You have long had a special claim on the past; now we have it too." I do not want here to pursue the question of who has the more authentic purchase on the past. Such questions uselessly distort our capacity for learning about that past. They depend on knowing with a high level of certainty what the past *is*—what the endeavor is seeking to capture or recover, how to recognize when a capture has succeeded, and how, in a scientific sense, to measure the capture's operation (almost like a fishing expedition: how many did you catch?)

Yet history's yield may be greatest when its limits are most clearly recognized. And documentary, as a particular cinematic mode, might illuminate historical inquiry most usefully by helping to elucidate those limits. For example, Bill Nichols's influential definition of documentary conjures a phenomenon not significantly different from the practice of history itself:

> Strategies and styles deployed in documentary, like those of narrative film, change; they have a history. And they have changed for much the same reasons: the dominant modes . . . change; the arena of ideological contestation shifts. The comfortably accepted realism of one generation seems like artifice to the next. New strategies must constantly be fabricated to re-present "things as they are" and still others to contest this very representation.[18]

Nichols suggests that the "contestation among forms" in documentary's evolution has "centered on the question of 'voice.'" And his conception of "voice" is very precise. Nichols calls it "something narrower than style: that which conveys to us a sense of a text's social point of view, of how it is speaking to us and how it is organizing the materials it is presenting to us." Voice, in this sense, "is not restricted to any one code or feature, such as dialogue or spoken commentary . . . [but] . . . is perhaps akin to that intangible, moirélike pattern formed by the unique interaction of all a film's codes. . . ."[19]

Dominick LaCapra enriches this notion of a film's—of any text's—internal chorus when he observes that it is easy to lose sight of the "way 'documents' are themselves texts that 'process' or rework 'reality' and require a critical reading that goes beyond traditional . . . forms."[20] Documentary films, which by their nature are more susceptible than other film forms to being physically "re-worked" and have traditionally been granted greater authority in representing the actual world, often acquire their authority through what we might call an "anti-rhetoric rhetoric."[21] That is, because of what they implicitly promise—to see the world as it is, unadorned—documentaries in effect compel us to judge them by the all-or-nothing standard of evidence that they provide—as either truths or lies. Yet it seems that we stand to gain much more from nonfiction films, as we do from historical accounts generally, if we read them with an eye to their implicit claims of verisimilitude as well as to their inevitable craft—for both documentary's reputation and presumed influence as a "discourse of sobriety," to borrow Nichols's phrase, depend heavily on our wishful belief, as spectators, that the mode is less clouded, less narratively "spun" than other cinematic forms of portrayal, and is thus more reliable than most media representations.[22]

Hollywood and its imitators have produced about past events countless entertaining movies whose popularity and influence owe much to both the pleasurable physical sensations and reassuring political and cultural narratives that such films traditionally have provided spectators. Indeed, Hollywood's expansive media system—the world's most dominant in manner of representation as well as mode of production—derives much of its power from its ability to exploit cinema as both *medium* and *mode*. As a material medium, Hollywood's movies have long dazzled with their radiant, groundbreaking technology and their visual spectacle. As a conceptual mode, such motion pictures have soothed—and often repressed—social anxieties by telling stories that are familiar in their use of a conventional emotional vernacular and that offer artificially heightened kinds of individual and collective resolution. Still, for all its popular appeal, this global mythmaking giant has often encountered sharp resistance when it has sought to depict actual events and experiences—when it has sought to be taken seriously as genuine historical representation.

In contrast to Hollywood's frequent entanglement in controversies about historical truthfulness and rigor, nonfiction cinema largely has remained apart from this antagonism, presumed, perhaps, to operate above the struggle for factual accuracy. But the "free pass" many traditional historians seem to have given documentary (whether out of unfounded respect or simple disinterest) only underscores the false dichotomy—the tension between so-called legitimate history and its inferior cinematic rival—that has come to characterize the general relationship between film and history. Champions of nonfiction film (whether spectators or filmmakers themselves), perhaps too enamored of the cinematic medium's ever advancing mechanical powers and the documentary mode's apparent capacity for truthful depiction, have often believed too much—too literally—in documentary's ability to give them "reality." Ironically, this critical tendency may render documentary a *more* useful mode than conventional narrative film for delving seriously into the problems inherent in depicting past events. The failure to treat documentary *as a mode*, a kind of window on reality that frames a particular, though incomplete, way of seeing, understanding, and believing, is a failure that pervades also the traditional practice of history.

In these ways, we who have embraced documentary so eagerly, so uncritically, have overlooked a more substantive, if complex, analogy for written history itself. For whether we attempt to portray and understand the actual world using the historian's pen or the filmmaker's camera, what has gone before is always, and forever, not actually with us. We know that time passed, that people were born and lived and fought and loved and died. But there is an important difference between saying that there exists a true or real or objective version of all of that and believing that we can actually *capture* it. Sometimes we who fashion historical accounts forget that the very enterprise depends on this gap, on our being removed from a reality that we can never fully apprehend: those bright, shining facts.[23]

The perspective I am endorsing here does not exempt us from the search for such facts, to be sure. But it does insist that we pay close attention to what is happening—to lives, relationships, beliefs, nations—in the *process* of building an account that is in any way based on those facts. That process itself is an important history, especially so if we are interested in the past because we believe, in one way or another, that it can instruct us and improve our lives now or in the future. In short, by studying documentary we may be able to learn more about our organic history—our evolving present—even if (or perhaps because) this means relinquishing the dream of a fixed, knowable past and thus opening our minds to the fundamental contingencies of both our lived experience and our attempts to represent it.[24]

With this in mind, we might ask what *Human Remains*—whether as history, as film, or as a film about history—has to teach us. History, if it is to be practiced (whether in popular or professional ways), needs a mechanism, a set of rules. Yet *Human Remains* appears to seek something real that challenges and defies familiar structures and forms. Had Ken Burns made *The Civil War* without any structures of time, space, or mortality, might he have produced a work exuding something of the uncertainty, the irresolution, of *Human Remains?*

Of course, we can reasonably question *Human Remains* as history. We might do better, however, to consider whether or how it is a documentary. The movie's techniques of a conspicuously manufactured sound track and alienating music; its use of biographical and autobiographical sources; its reworking of footage; its striking use of "negatives"; its selection of bodily, highly personal, but unappealing anecdotes—these and other formal devices all work against conventions of the "real" and play with our expectations as documentary-familiar spectators. Dirk Eitzen argues that the most meaningful measure of a film's documentary character is its susceptibility to the question "might it be lying?" Thus for Eitzen, the guiding question is not "*what* is a documentary?" but rather, "*when* is a documentary?"[25] And so we must ask whether it is this spectatorial anticipation, this attitude of expectation, that *Human Remains* engages as it weaves its provocative web of possible meanings.

Does Eitzen's question (might it be lying?) apply to *Human Remains?* Surely Rosenblatt wants his audience to ask the question; he structures his movie as a pastiche of the conventional interview documentary. Rosenblatt has claimed that all the characters' statements in the film were drawn from authenticated sources. But the movie nonetheless creates the (fairly transparent) fiction that these are actual interviews, made postmortem (perhaps in hell, as suggested by the shoveler or "gravedigger," as the closing credits identify him, or by the Irving Berlin song—"When That Man Is Dead and Gone"—that plays under those credits). Hitler's indignant claim, in the film, that photographs in which he appeared with pets and children were "propaganda—pure and simple!"; Stalin's suggestion that Lenin's enshrined body was a fake; Franco's explicit recognition that he is speaking of his own past, from beyond the grave; Mao's admission that his public appearances were staged—these all overload, as it were, one of documentary's best-known forms, one of its most *traditional* forms, in order to provoke reflection on the inexplicability of history, on how men such as these were able to realize such enormous damage.[26]

After an early screening of the film, Rosenblatt said that he imagined his work as a "return of the repressed," an example of a century's media avenging its own iconography.[27] It is in this stylized vengeance that *Human Remains* achieves its greatest power. Watching it, like watching any movie, is only the lived experience of watching a movie. Reading a book or observing a photograph also is, first and foremost, the lived experience of reading a book or observing a photograph. No film, then, or documentary, is about actually recapturing the lived experience of a different time and place but of reading or observing a representation that is its *own* lived experience—a way to engage with or consider previous lived experiences in a way that is somehow useful.[28]

In the lived experience of watching and listening to *Human Remains*, manifold voices arise, their gratuitous relation obscured at first by the archival icons that command our view: Hitler, Mussolini, Stalin, Mao, Franco. But as the awkward intimacy of unseemly personal detail takes hold, the voices are suddenly strange as well. Familiar to us only in the structured exchange of photographs, documents, newsreels, television programs, they now appear to be something different. The film's deceptively complex sound track compounds their strangeness. As the dictators appear in succession, English voice-overs cover and translate their German, Italian, Russian, Spanish, and Mandarin declarations. Yet these original-language utterances are not actual recordings of the protagonists' words; they are contemporary original language voice-over reenactments, themselves then covered by contemporary English voice-overs.

What is the purpose of these tricky, double-layered voice-overs? While to the English-speaking spectator's ear they may at first seem a reasonable translation strategy, they are unnecessary for any literal comprehension of the film. As it progresses they cast a murky, even troubling shadow. The indulgent layering of voice-overs is a highly self-reflexive gesture, a rebuke of the notion that translation—whether linguistic or historical—follows logical rules, and a reminder that "Hitler" and his fellow dictators, in addition to having existed as actual human beings, are to us significantly a product of what others say about them—characters structured by multiple voices.

In this and other ways equally impossible to ignore, *Human Remains* deploys elaborate production strategies that challenge spectators' presumed familiarity with its leading men. Although known primarily as martial heads of state, the dictators never appear in official military uniform. Visually stripped of some of their best-known signifiers of power, the men seem somehow alien, even though all the images Rosenblatt uses are archival. Deploying newsreel and archival footage (materials through which the men are recognizable and not physically reenacted), then, Rosenblatt fashions a sequence of odd profiles that are at once historically accurate and absurdly (sometimes comically) ordinary.

This method draws attention to the incongruity between lived experience and intellectual form.[29] In fact, Rosenblatt's manipulation of the film medium, coupled with his interrogation of the documentary mode, erodes conventional distinctions between experience and form, leaving us to wonder whether *Human Remains,* an apparently historical

GEOFF PINGREE

documentary, is not more a documentary about—even a documentary *of*—history.[30]

So in representing Hitler and other tyrants, *Human Remains* probes not only the genre of documentary but also the nature of history itself. The film's five dictators are central players in many of the last century's greatest horrors. Yet the movie steps away from these characters' well-documented legacies of violence and destruction, focusing instead on their stunning lack of self-awareness. However different from one another they may have been in life, Rosenblatt teases out certain themes that unite them: an obsession with bodily functions and the sometimes strange hygiene practices employed to tame them; an appreciation of the sensual appeal of the foods they love ("chocolate éclairs," says Hitler, his voice quivering) and hate; and a perspective on sex—often aberrant—that is oddly detached.

Rendering these monstrous giants' lives strangely pedestrian, often in their own words, the film seems to wonder if their atrocities stem from emptiness, banality, and nothingness. Despite some memorably humorous confessions and shared physiological oddities (e.g., one testicle), these tyrants' "remains" raise unusual questions about the peculiarity of evil. *Human Remains* itself seems more than anything else concerned with our mediated understanding of these men as emblems of history, as the grand movers responsible for many of the last century's most horrible realities.

With his film, then, Rosenblatt makes a case that recalls Hannah Arendt's *Eichmann in Jerusalem*. Arendt famously subtitled her work "A Report on the Banality of Evil" not because Eichmann's actions led to no evil (he was considered the architect of the Nazis' "final solution"), nor because the consequences of his actions were banal, but because a careful look at the man on trial, and his life and experience, did not add up to a monster—a being of a different species, a man *other* than ourselves.

In Arendt's view, the facts about Eichmann pointed instead to an everyman, an inexplicable figure who did not exhibit the sensational traits of a psychopathic killer. Eichmann instead embodied something that, for those seeking a hard and clear narrative of justice, was far less satisfying: a man of limited ability and attention, a man devoid of grand purpose. By acknowledging Eichmann's ordinariness, Arendt undermined those who, in bringing him to trial, were determined not only to punish but to explain—to find a cause for—the dreadful events he had helped set in motion. In her account, Arendt thus stripped of its predetermined dramatic arc the story that was being told in the Jerusalem courtroom. She extracted from the history Eichmann represented its seemingly indisputable causal framework.[31]

In *Human Remains* Rosenblatt, like Arendt, steps outside established, systematic modes of seeing and depicting, usurping generic conventions in a way that compels us to ask what it is that we seek from history, particularly in a moral sense. *Human Remains* brings its characters to trial, but it presents facts that accentuate the essential inexplicability of the men's behavior. And for all the ways in which the film hints at the degree to which Hitler, Stalin, and the rest are unknown to themselves, *Human Remains* presents us, the audience, with the far more consequential mystery of how to meaningfully link these individuals to the gruesome history they made. In this, the movie also obliges us to ponder the nature of evil itself.

What cultural context could have enabled men of such cruelty to affect so many people? To make some sense of this question, the film encourages us to relinquish a strictly causal notion of history and to consider instead—ironically—a flatter, more two-dimensional narrative model. The non-verbal elements of the sound track (low, notably dark, brooding, electric, and never-ceasing—what we might call the "sound of inexplicability") buttress this attitude. This view both lines up and clashes with the film's explanatory statements (that don't really explain) and with the apparently actual, synchronously recorded ambient sounds we occasionally hear. Dismantling and demystifying (but not reconstructing) totalitarian icons of twentieth-century history by reducing or returning them to pedestrian, even quotidian, lives of earthy details, idiosyncrasies, and fetishes, the movie raises the unsettling possibility that—if we are honest—"information" finally explains little or nothing.

Together these techniques—the mysterious use of voices and sound, the reworked images, even the close-ups of running train tracks that open and close the film—pose a key question: what is the most *useful*, representational way to contend with the horror that suffuses history? Rosenblatt's innovative strategies seem to ask how the lived experience of one kind of representation might engage with the traumatic lived experiences of those no longer with us—experiences that we can only imagine. This kind of engagement with the past, what we might call "suggestively empathic" history, generates a wholly different calculus for measuring historical inquiry, an evaluative method that enables what surely must count as meaningful historical understanding.

Rather than disparage traditional historical methods, *Human Remains* proposes a distinct, *differently* worthwhile style of engaging with the past. This approach more consciously acknowledges that in producing history we are working with representations of the past. It is a style that struggles to understand what the past means or can mean, to be sure, but a style that also considers how our contingent perceptions of the actual world shape those meanings. It recognizes too that the ways we experience representations are themselves part of the meaning-making process. The reworked footage, the altered speed of motion, and the fluid images all contribute to a genuinely innovative view, and viewing experience, of too-familiar media icons. Indeed, the film is empowered by an emphasis on form and medium—on the conceptual and material nature of cinema itself and on its own specificity *as media*.[32]

By humanizing its characters, toying with its conventions of authenticity, shuffling its contexts, playing with its archival materials, and highlighting—almost mocking—its reliance on the material nature of motion pictures, *Human Remains* powerfully questions the nature of historical characters, the possibility of historical authenticity, the influence of historical context, the use of historical archives, and the prospect of history on film. By encouraging us to see the past in genuinely new ways, the movie seems to embody Nichols's suggestion that documentary cinema "operates in the crease between life as lived and life as narrativised."[33]

We study history as if we could know it. But there will be no final consensus on what has gone before, and the only understanding we will fully, easily share is that time has passed, is passing, will pass. The dead cannot answer any more than we, once dead, can speak for ourselves. Yet we have no choice but to answer for them. Such answering is what we *can* do. But for all its limitations, this answering, what we call "history," is what abides. It is what we talk about; it is what stands for what has passed. History is neither the static remains nor the reliable evidence of something so much as it is a process of searching: what we are able to do, what we choose to do. As Franco—unwittingly, astutely—declares upon departing the film, "How hard it is to die."[34]

NOTES

1. *Human Remains*, dir. Jay Rosenblatt (Denmark: Transit Media, 1998).

2. Here I must make reference to Walter Benjamin's well-known 1936 discussion of "aura." Walter Benjamin, "The Work of Art in the Age of Mechanical Reproduction," in *Illuminations* (New York: Schocken, 1969), 217–52. All five of the dictators in *Human Remains*, having exploited diverse means of mechanical reproduction and mass media to enlarge their influence in ways barely imaginable before the twentieth century, seemed to invite what would surely be instructive examination of themselves as self-created icons, generators of a style of political power that appears to borrow much from the grand traditions of aesthetic representation with which

Benjamin contends. It is as if Rosenblatt's film were conscious of the contradictions Benjamin identified between the unique, immediate, intimate quality—the aura—of earlier, individually created works of art and the common, pervasive, redundant character of cinema and other mass media. Presenting political figures who fabricated images of themselves that would reach large audiences and, in effect, transform spectators' inveterate reverence into modern awe, *Human Remains* articulates paradoxes of the modern condition in unsettling and distinctly Benjaminian ways. The German cultural theorist was clearly aware, after all, that even though it obliterated traditional aura, mass media—especially cinema—could enable the type of social propaganda necessary for the formation of authoritarian ideologies and regimes. By focusing on the intimate, private details of its characters' actual lives, *Human Remains* subtly underscores the difference between a traditional aesthetic aura and modern political charisma. And by working within the tradition of the documentary film, Rosenblatt seems to strike at the heart of Benjamin's concerns, foregrounding the evolving relations between art and technology, politics and representation. In the years when Rosenblatt's dictators were gaining political supremacy, documentary cinema, as Bill Nichols notes, largely had become a political instrument, a mode used primarily to affirm or contest the "power of the state." Bill Nichols, "Documentary Film and the Modernist Avant-Garde," *Critical Inquiry* 27 (Summer 2001): 582. Indeed, *Human Remains* illustrates Nichols's observation that documentary films can situate the "historical person in recognizable tension with myths and stereotypes which evade the claims of historical contingency and human mortality." Bill Nichols, *Representing Reality: Issues and Concepts in Documentary* (Bloomington: Indiana University Press, 1991), xv.

3. Here I am employing David Bordwell and Kristin Thompson's precise notion of *narration* in the narrative film as the "process through which the *plot* conveys or withholds *story* information." Bordwell and Thompson contend that while *plot* comprises only "the events . . . directly presented to us . . . ," *story* includes "all of the events that we see and hear, plus all those that we infer or assume to have occurred." David Bordwell and Kristin Thompson, *Film Art: An Introduction*, 7th ed. (New York: McGraw-Hill, 2004), 504–5.

4. My address, "Modern Anxiety: Documentary Cinema, Social Reform, and the Second Republic," and Nelson's remarks, were part of an interdisciplinary symposium, "Recalcitrant Modernities: Spain, Difference, and the Construction of European Modernism," held 26–27 September 2003 at the University of Illinois at Urbana-Champaign.

5. After decades of enforced suppression, memory of what happened between 1936–39, the civil war years, and during the brutal dictatorship that followed, has awakened in Spain with a vengeance. Indeed, the so-called Pact of Silence—which effectively forbid any mention of the horrors of the war and dictatorship while the country transformed itself into a democracy—has given way in recent years to a rising cacophony of controversial demands to revisit, and recover, the past. Multiple organizations hunt and unearth mass graves of those executed during the war, file legal challenges to clear names and win reparations for the descendants of those persecuted, and question the entire legal system erected by Franco's regime. Bookstores are lined with new works that chronicle the barbarities of the war and the dictatorship, and barely a month goes by without the release of a new documentary film on the subject. Cities across Spain are debating whether to change street names—the Avenidas del Generalísimo and Plazas de José Antonio Primo de

GEOFF PINGREE

Rivera—that still celebrate the Franco regime. The current government, which has established a special commission to recognize and compensate the dictatorship's victims, has authorized the removal of Madrid's last statue of the dictator, and Congress has approved a plan to return to Catalonia documents held in the central government's civil war archives, a collection originally taken from the region by Franco's advancing armies.

6. George Orwell, "Looking Back on the Spanish War," in *The Collected Essays, Journalism, and Letters of George Orwell*, vol. 2, edited by Sonia Orwell and Ian Angus, 256–58 (New York: Harcourt, 1968).

7. Francis Fukuyama, *The End of History and the Last Man* (New York: Harper-Collins, 1993).

8. Kenneth Burke, *Attitudes toward History*, 3rd ed. (Berkeley: University of California Press, 1984).

9. I further discuss Orwell's remarks in my PhD dissertation, "Forging Witnesses: Rhetorics of Documentary Representation in the Spanish Civil War" (University of Chicago, 1996).

10. Broad discussions of the development of, and relations among, different models of history are plentiful. Two useful examples, from different periods in academic historiography, are Edward Hallett Carr, *What Is History?* (New York: Vintage, 1961) and Joyce Appleby, Lynn Hunt, and Margaret Jacob, *Telling the Truth about History* (New York: Norton, 1994). Explorations of the tension between objective ideals and subjective experience are perhaps more abundant. From distinct fields, two that focus intelligently on this tension as it relates to narrative representation are Richard Rorty, *Irony, Contingency, and Solidarity* (Cambridge: Cambridge University Press, 1989) and Honi Fern Haber, *Beyond Postmodern Politics: Selves, Community, and a Politics of Difference* (New York: Taylor & Francis, 1994).

11. For a persuasive discussion of "ideal-regarding" methods of analysis and interpretation, see Christopher Butler, "On the Rivalry of Norms for Interpretation," *New Literary History* 20 (Autumn 1988): 123–39.

12. Jürgen Habermas grapples with the import of this wish when he writes, famously, that "our first sentence expresses unequivocally the intention of universal and unconstrained consensus." Jürgen Habermas, *Knowledge and Human Interests*, trans. Jeremy J. Shapiro (Boston: Beacon, 1971), 314. Indeed, among his many contributions to contemporary thought, few are more important than Habermas' effort to find a way to analyze social discourse that "offers an alternative to deconstruction without reproducing Enlightenment errors." Jürgen Habermas, *The Philosophical Discourse of Modernity*, trans. Frederick G. Lawrence (Cambridge: The MIT Press, 1990), 311.

13. Although it confirmed the collective regard for film's power, Rudolf Arnheim's essay "The Complete Film" expressed deep anxiety about art's future in the face of cinema's rapidly developing technology (Arnheim wrote the essay in 1933, when color film was but a few years old). At one point he wondered, fearfully, "What will the color film have to offer when it reaches *technical perfection?*" Rudolf Arnheim, "The Complete Film," in *Film Theory and Criticism*, ed. Leo Braudy and Marshall Cohen, 5th ed. (New York: Oxford University Press, 1999), 212, emphasis mine.

14. Richard Barry, "Five-Dollar Movies Prophesied: D. W. Griffith Says They Are Sure to Come with the Remarkable Advance in Film Productions," *New York Times Magazine*, 28 March 1915, 16, quoted in Donald F. Stevens, "Never Read History Again? The Possibilities and Perils of Cinema as Historical Depiction," in *Based*

on a True Story: Latin American History at the Movies (Wilmington, DE: SR Books, 1997), 1-2.

15. Virtually every film history or textbook in some way addresses early cinema's scientific aspirations. Two interesting examples where documentary is concerned are Erik Barnouw, *Documentary: A History of the Non-Fiction Film* (New York: Oxford University Press, 1974) and Richard Meran Barsam, *Nonfiction Film: A Critical History*, rev. ed. (Bloomington: Indiana University Press, 1992).

16. For further discussion of the complex relationship between the conceptual and material dimensions of new media, see, for example, James Lastra, *Sound Technology and the American Cinema: Perception, Representation, Modernity* (New York: Columbia University Press, 2000) or Lisa Gitelman and Geoffrey B. Pingree, eds., *New Media, 1740-1915* (Cambridge: The MIT Press, 2003).

17. One might argue, in fact, that history's dual concerns for protocol and meaning are, ultimately, inseparable.

18. Bill Nichols, "The Voice of Documentary," in *New Challenges for Documentary*, ed. Alan Rosenthal (Berkeley: University of California Press, 1988), 48.

19. Nichols, "The Voice of Documentary," 50.

20. Dominick LaCapra, *History and Criticism* (Ithaca: Cornell University Press, 1985), 19.

21. Whereas so-called fiction films effectively declare their intention openly to utilize creative formal and technical strategies in order to achieve compelling dramatic effects, documentaries, as we call them, manufacture their messages and stories more subtly, and within a context of different expectations, thus working under an umbrella of assurances—largely unspoken by both producers and audiences—of truthful depiction. Nichols suggests that often documentaries' "sense of urgency brushes aside our efforts to contemplate form or analyze rhetoric," so that even as they "offer pleasure and appeal . . . their own structure remains virtually invisible, their own rhetorical strategies and stylistic choices largely unnoticed." Nichols, *Representing Reality*, x.

22. Nichols believes that such discourses are "seldom receptive to 'make-believe' characters, events, or entire worlds (unless they serve as pragmatically useful simulations of the 'real' one)" and that they "are sobering because they regard their relation to the real as direct, immediate, transparent." He is quick to note, however, that documentary "is but another part of cinema, perhaps all the more devious for claiming to be above the deceptive means with which it makes its point (moving images)." Nichols, *Representing Reality*, 3-4.

23. Reflecting on documentary as history, Nichols reminds us that "what the documentarist cannot fully control is his or her basic subject: *history*. By addressing the historical domain, the documentarist joins the company of other practitioners who 'lack control' over what they do. . . . The notion of control as a defining criterion perpetuates a muddleheadedness about documentary filmmaking scarcely less egregious than claims for the truth of documentary representation or for the self-evidence of facts" (Nichols, *Representing Reality*, 14, emphasis mine).

24. The "separation between an image and what it refers to continues to be a difference that makes a difference," observes Nichols, adding that "our access to historical reality may only be by means of representations, and these representations may sometimes seem to be more eager to chase their own tails than able to guarantee the authenticity of what they refer to. Neither of these conditions, however, precludes the persistence of history as a reality with which we must contend. . . .

The reality of pain and loss that is not part of any simulation, in fact, is what makes the difference between representation and historical reality of crucial importance. It is not beyond the power of documentary to make this difference available for our consideration" (Nichols, *Representing Reality*, 7).

25. Dirk Eitzen, "When Is a Documentary?: Documentary as a Mode of Reception," *Cinema Journal* 35, no. 1 (Fall 1995): 81.

26. *Human Remains*, 1998.

27. Jay Rosenblatt, interview with the author, 25 May 1998. It may be worth noting that Rosenblatt is also a practicing psychotherapist.

28. Here I am influenced by, and playing on, some of Robert Rosenstone's ideas about the relations between film and history. See, for example, chapter 1 in *Visions of the Past: The Challenge of Film to Our Idea of History* (Cambridge: Harvard University Press, 1995) and the introduction to *Revisioning History: Film and the Construction of a New Past* (Princeton: Princeton University Press, 1995).

29. As Nichols puts it: "History—embodied, corporeal history—is at odds with narrative and myth." Bill Nichols, "History, Myth, and Narrative in Documentary," *Film Quarterly* 41 (Fall 1987): 16.

30. Nichols argues that it was only during the "1920s and early 1930s"—a politically formative period central to Rosenblatt's characters and concerns in *Human Remains*—that film as "document" (a purportedly static resource *for* history) became film as "documentary" (an unavoidably active reworking *of* history). Nichols explains that the latter, the documentary film as we know it today, emerged as "an actual practice" only once it combined four elements: "photographic realism, narrative structure, . . . modernist fragmentation [and an] . . . emphasis on the rhetoric of social persuasion." Nichols, "Documentary Film and the Modernist Avant-Garde," 582.

31. Hannah Arendt, *Eichmann in Jerusalem: A Report on the Banality of Evil*, rev. ed. (New York: Penguin, 1979).

32. I consider "media specificity," a notion widely discussed in cinema and media studies, to rest primarily on a concern with *how* things mean, rather than simply *what* they mean or *why*. Such an approach considers a text's material nature (as well as its conceptual content) to account for what and how that text can mean. In Nichols' words, "Signifiers come with images attached. They *are* images, and sounds, and they are always concrete, material, and specific. What films have to say about the enduring human condition or about the pressing issues of the day can never be separated from *how* they say it, how this saying moves and affects us, how we engage with a work, not with a theory of it" (Nichols, *Representing Reality*, xiii).

33. Quoted in Brian Winston, *Claiming the Real: The Documentary Film Revisited*, (London: British Film Institute, 1995), 101.

34. *Human Remains*, 1998.

REFERENCES

Appleby, Joyce, Lynn Hunt, and Margaret Jacob. *Telling the Truth about History*. New York: Norton, 1994.

Arendt, Hannah. *Eichmann in Jerusalem: A Report on the Banality of Evil*. Rev. ed. New York: Penguin, 1979.

Arnheim, Rudolf. "The Complete Film." In *Film Theory and Criticism*, edited by Leo Braudy and Marshall Cohen, 212–15. 5th ed. New York: Oxford University Press, 1999.

Barnouw, Erik. *Documentary: A History of the Non-Fiction Film*. New York: Oxford University Press, 1974.

Barry, Richard. "Five-Dollar Movies Prophesied: D. W. Griffith Says They Are Sure to Come with the Remarkable Advance in Film Productions." *New York Times Magazine*, 28 March 1915, 16. Quoted in Donald F. Stevens, "Never Read History Again? The Possibilities and Perils of Cinema as Historical Depiction." In *Based on a True Story: Latin American History at the Movies*, 1–11. Wilmington, DE: SR Books, 1997.

Barsam, Richard Meran. *Nonfiction Film: A Critical History*. Rev. ed. Bloomington: Indiana University Press, 1992.

Benjamin, Walter. "The Work of Art in the Age of Mechanical Reproduction." In *Illuminations*, 217–52. New York: Schocken, 1969.

Bordwell, David, and Kristin Thompson. *Film Art: An Introduction*. 7th ed. New York: McGraw-Hill, 2004.

Burke, Kenneth. *Attitudes toward History*. 3rd ed. Berkeley: University of California Press, 1984.

Butler, Christopher. "On the Rivalry of Norms for Interpretation." *New Literary History* 20 (Autumn 1988): 123–39.

Carr, Edward Hallett. *What Is History?* New York: Vintage, 1961.

Eitzen, Dirk. "When Is a Documentary?: Documentary as a Mode of Reception." *Cinema Journal* 35, no. 1 (Fall 1995): 81–102.

Fukuyama, Francis. *The End of History and the Last Man*. New York: HarperCollins, 1993.

Gitelman, Lisa, and Geoffrey B. Pingree, eds. *New Media, 1740–1915*. Cambridge: The MIT Press, 2003.

Haber, Honi Fern. *Beyond Postmodern Politics: Selves, Community, and a Politics of Difference*. New York: Taylor & Francis, 1994.

Habermas, Jürgen. *Knowledge and Human Interests*. Trans. Jeremy J. Shapiro. Boston: Beacon Press, 1971.

———. *The Philosophical Discourse of Modernity*. Trans. Frederick G. Lawrence. Cambridge: The MIT Press, 1990.

Human Remains. Dir. Jay Rosenblatt. Denmark: Transit Media, 1998.

LaCapra, Dominick. *History and Criticism*. Ithaca: Cornell University Press, 1985.

Lastra, James. *Sound Technology and the American Cinema: Perception, Representation, Modernity*. New York: Columbia University Press, 2000.

Nichols, Bill. "Documentary Film and the Modernist Avant-Garde." *Critical Inquiry* 27 (Summer 2001): 580–610.

———. "History, Myth and Narrative in Documentary." *Film Quarterly* 41 (Fall 1987): 9–12.

———. *Representing Reality: Issues and Concepts in Documentary*. Bloomington: Indiana University Press, 1991.

———. "The Voice of Documentary." In *New Challenges for Documentary*, 48–63. Ed. Alan Rosenthal. Berkeley: University of California Press, 1988.

Orwell, George. "Looking Back on the Spanish War." In *The Collected Essays, Journalism, and Letters of George Orwell*, 249–67. volume 2, edited by Sonia Orwell and Ian Angus. New York: Harcourt, 1968.

Pingree, Geoffrey B. "Forging Witnesses: Rhetorics of Documentary Representation in the Spanish Civil War." PhD diss., University of Chicago, 1996.

———. "Modern Anxiety: Documentary Cinema, Social Reform, and the Second

Republic." Paper delivered at the "Recalcitrant Modernities: Spain, Difference, and the Construction of European Modernism" symposium, University of Illinois at Urbana-Champaign, 26 September 2003.

Rorty, Richard. *Contingency, Irony, and Solidarity.* Cambridge: Cambridge University Press, 1989.

Rosenblatt, Jay. Interview with the author. 25 May 1998.

Rosenstone, Robert A. *Visions of the Past: The Challenge of Film to Our Idea of History.* Cambridge: Harvard University Press, 1995.

————, ed. *Revisioning History: Film and the Construction of a New Past.* Princeton: Princeton University Press, 1995.

Winston, Brian. *Claiming the Real: The Documentary Film Revisited.* London: British Film Institute, 1995.

CRUSADERS AND SARACENS
THE PERSISTENCE OF ORIENTALISM
IN HISTORICALLY THEMED MOTION
PICTURES ABOUT THE MIDDLE EAST
····

RICHARD FRANCAVIGLIA

Two conflicting forces square off when history is depicted on the silver screen. First, the serious filmmaker endeavors to *inform* the audience about what happened—or what is thought to have happened. This might include reference to particular dates or the accurate wording of a speech that was given on that documented date. Even though that understanding may be contested by historians, we still might call it the *intellectual* part of the dynamic. However, a second factor also enters the equation, because the filmmaker must *appeal* to the public's expectations about how the time period "felt." Can the filmmaker convey the feelings of terror and elation of war and victory? The gloom of an economic depression? This is the *emotional* side of the equation, and it plays an equal, and sometimes larger, part in how a film treats the past. This emotional side is further complicated by the filmmaker's desire to dramatize—and possibly make judgments about—what happened.

Consider, for example, how a filmmaker in the 1950s might portray an important political/military event like the rise of Genghis Khan. Students of history in film have just such an opportunity by studying Howard Hughes' *The Conqueror* (1956), which offers both a sobering and humorous example of how Hollywood treated epic history on an epic scale in the 1950s. The film's locale is Mongolia during the 1200s, but the Cold War made shooting on location entirely out of the question. This dilemma more or less necessitated filming closer to home, in Utah to be more exact. Then, too, because movie studios believed that a film had to feature easily recognized movie stars, and those stars were Caucasian, *The Conqueror* succumbed to some legendary miscasting: envision John

Wayne as Temujin, the Mongol who ultimately attains the title of Geng-his Khan. If this selection seems odd, imagine the shapely, red-haired, green-eyed beauty Susan Hayward as Bortai, a Tartar princess. As if to introduce some ethnic authenticity, Pedro Armendariz plays Timugen's brother, but his Spanish-flavored English is as odd as the stiff lines that all the characters voice in this epic.

The Conqueror was produced toward the end of that golden period in which films began with a bow to the written word, often a page or more of text to set the scene historically. Text like this scrolls upward as it informs viewers about the period, location, events, and characters. *The Conqueror* begins with an enigmatic written disclaimer just before such textual wording appears: "This story, though fiction, is based on fact." That disclaimer is ambitious in that the facts are only vaguely determinable in the film, which is mostly conjectural. Nevertheless, it suggests that many, if not most, historically themed films might employ a version of it: "This story, though supposedly factual, is based on fiction." The fiction, of course, is the conjecture that the filmmakers introduce concerning geographic locale, artifacts, and—most importantly—dialogue and motive. The additional text appearing on the screen at the opening of *The Conqueror* provides an overview of the period in which barbarians stormed across the Asian steppe—a time of treachery when "brother could not trust brother" and "rapine" was common. This wording provides a simplistic overview of complex events, but it prepares the viewer/reader for the drama about to take place. In a deeply subliminal sense, it harks back to the Old Testament times of Cain and Abel, and the barbaric times depicted in paintings like "The Rape of the Sabine Women."

Reading words like these, we sense that we are about to witness some genuine betrayal and mayhem. As *The Conqueror*'s introductory wording loosely sets the historical background, the desert landscape "sets the scene" as the Asian steppe. From the left of the screen we hear the increasing crescendo of hoofbeats just as the camera moves left to catch a thundering herd of riders on horseback that flashes across the screen from left to right as the words THE CONQUEROR take up the full screen.

Like most films set in the distant past in distant places, *The Conqueror* required sweeping desert vistas to authenticate its barbarian promise. As *The Conqueror*'s director, Dick Powell faced the challenge of portraying an isolated desert region halfway around the world almost a thousand years ago. Despite his best effort, Powell wound up giving both Mongolia and Mongolians the strangely familiar look of the old American West. There is something familiar about the way Wayne rides his Mongolian horse, for he had done it in numerous westerns. Then, too, that

Princess Bortai (Susan Hayward) and Temujin (John Wayne). From The Conqueror *(RKO Radio Pictures, 1956; courtesy Photofest)*

landscape looks awfully familiar because the spectacular Utah desert doubles as the Gobi. The filmmaker's use of Utah for Mongolia was easy to excuse: despite Utah's familiarity, virtually no viewer but a geographer would sense any *real* miscasting here because, viewers were unsure and could be easily convinced that the Gobi looks just like what they were seeing on-screen. This is a reminder that all audiences—popular or academic—are remarkably unaware of geography—probably even more unaware than they are of history. The filmmakers of the period further conspired to keep their "exotic" locale secret by not revealing the locations in the credits.

The Conqueror is widely known as a career killer because the film's cast reportedly succumbed to cancer in disproportionate numbers. That has been attributed to nearby nuclear testing (even the hauling in of radioactive Utah dirt to the Hollywood soundstage where part of the film was shot), but this colorful interpretation is largely apocryphal and more in the category of an urban legend. This environmental explanation somehow overlooks Wayne's three-pack-a-day habit and his subsequent death from lung cancer two decades *after* the filming. But *The Conqueror,* which is regarded by some critics as the worst historical epic ever shot by Hollywood, needed *something* to distinguish it, and nuclear testing may help to explain its status as both killer and bomb.[1]

I began this essay by highlighting *The Conqueror* because it typifies so many American films that portray the exotic, southwestern Asian deserts, and the people who inhabit them, as barbaric and sensual. For example, when Wayne and his fellow tribesmen ogle a sensuous dancing woman at a gathering, we learn that she is from Samarkand. The salacious words that "compared to such women from Samarkand, all others are like the second pressing of the grape" reveals just how much fantasy can go into a historical epic. But *The Conqueror* was meant to be taken seriously as a film about Asia, and it has all the elements we commonly associate with the East—wisdom and stupidity, bravery and cowardice, opulence and poverty, kindness and torture. But films about another part of the East—the Middle East—are the ones that I would like to discuss in greater detail. Like *The Conqueror,* these films depict a region and the peoples who inhabited it in times past. In the Middle East, however, the stakes are higher, because the region was, and is, central to three religions that continue to coexist, if uneasily at times. Unlike the way we experience *The Conqueror,* however, we take these films more seriously because they are about a serious subject—religion.

THE MIDDLE EAST:
BIRTHPLACE OF JUDEO-CHRISTIAN TRADITIONS

For more than two millennia, the Middle East has been central to the debate about mankind's relationship with God and, especially, humankind's tendency to find absolute answers in an environment of shifting sands and shimmering mirages. Because three great religions developed here, the region has been an ideological battleground for much of that period. In the century since motion pictures were introduced, filmmaking has become the most effective way to dramatize stories about such conflicts for large audiences. Given the enduring interest in stories that dramatize religious history—for example, the recent blockbuster success of *The Passion of the Christ*—it is not surprising that film has depicted some of the Middle East's greatest mythological and historical events. Despite the logistical difficulties in filming those events, filmmakers have taken cameras and casts into desert places in hopes of capturing on celluloid the powerful stories associated with this region. Although Westerners consider the Middle East exotic, we are nevertheless familiar with it because we have read so much about it in the Torah, the Bible, and the Quoran.

Of the many film genres, films about the Middle East most often fit into categories of religion, war, drama, and adventure. As suggested above, capturing events that transpired in the Old World deserts, namely a huge arid area from North Africa to western Pakistan, has been among the most difficult, and controversial, ventures that a filmmaker can undertake. The list of historically themed Old World desert films is fairly large and includes some of the classics in religious spectacle (such as *The Ten Commandments*) and political intrigue (for example, *Lawrence of Arabia*). The genre continues into the present with the recent *Hidalgo* (2003) and Ridley Scott's spectacular film *Kingdom of Heaven* (2005). The latter is also in the genre of the religious epic—one that depicts the power of a religious movement or ideology through some crucial event or events.

Like all films intended for general audiences, these religious epics entertain by simplifying complexity, reducing ambiguity, and giving order to chaos. Their generally smooth camera work, easy-to-follow story lines, and aesthetic imagery suggest a comprehensible desert world undergoing linear change. Good and evil are pretty much recognizable, and situations are fairly clear. This is true of popular films depicting the birth of the region's three major religions: Judaism, Christianity, and Islam. The story lines and casting of Charlton Heston as Moses in *The Ten Commandments* (1956) and Max von Sydow as Jesus in *The Greatest Story Ever Told* (1965) present images that are storybook perfect. In the more image-sensitive Islamic world, visual depictions of religious figures are approached far more cautiously. Take, for example, *The Message* (1976), an intriguing film about the creation of Islam from the tribal miasma of Arabia at that pivotal time—circa 615 A.D.—when Muhammad became "the Messenger of God." In *The Message,* the prophet Muhammad offers a compelling solution to the idolatry and depravity of the Arab world at that time, where slavery was commonplace, gods innumerable, and women devalued. But in this film, which was made with Islamic audiences in mind, Muhammad had to be treated nonvisually, or rather invisibly. For reasons of religious sensitivity/appreciation, he is *never* actually shown, yet he is absolutely central to the film's plot. In a masterful use of presence-by-absence, Muhammad here is larger than life. We never see him, but we glimpse his sword and see people's expressions when they behold him. Nor do we ever *hear* him speak. In fact, we only know Muhammad through the *words* he records as the Quran—words that are read by a narrator or voiced by others. In *The Message,* Anthony Quinn is the prophet's surrogate—the quintessential desert dweller who is mobile, wise, strong, passionate, mercurial, familial, and brave. Motivated by Muhammad, and hence God, he joins the fight for religious freedom and social justice with complete honor, even magnanimity, and is ultimately martyred.[2]

These religious desert epics require a spectacular stage because the story of the religions themselves is so intimately associated with two types of environments—the *desert*, with its expanses of sandy and rocky barren land, and the *village*, with its grouping of individuals and families, who by turns support and thwart the messages of the prophets, whether they be Moses, Jesus, or Muhammad. This contrast is seminal to *all* religious desert dramas. The story is familiar. Religious leaders receive inspiration from God in these desert wilderness places, with their barren mountains, deep canyons, and vast expanses of sand. After recording or memorizing the lessons, however, they must implement the word of God in the imperfect places where men dwell—places full of distractions like the prospects of wealth and the pleasures of the flesh.

Like the hapless star-turned-director Dick Powell of *The Conqueror* fame (or infamy), filmmakers of such epics search carefully for dramatic geographic locales in which to represent this dichotomy. In their quest, they too look for places that either make the drama credible or enhance its emotional impact. Like Powell, their choices are affected not only by aesthetic conditions but also by funding and politics. Interestingly, the Middle East is such a volatile place—or rather we might say that the actual locale associated with the founding of these three religions is so contested and defended—that *actual* locales are rarely or never used. This explains why Morocco, Libya, and Jordan doubled for Arabia during the politically tense early 1960s (*The Message, Lawrence of Arabia*); Pyramid Lake, Nevada, doubled for the Sea of Galilee when war threatened to break out between Israel and the Arab world in the mid-1960s (*The Greatest Story Every Told*); and the Mojave Desert doubled for off-limits Arabia and Syria in a dramatization of a cross-desert horse race filmed in 2003 (*Hidalgo*). That the Holy Land had become too hot a locale, politically speaking, for filming is evident in the locations selected to film the *Kingdom of Heaven*—Spain and Morocco. The presence of Spain is quite interesting here for that was the location of a film about the spread of Islam into the Iberian Peninsula in the eleventh century, *El Cid* (1961).

Whereas an epic film like *El Cid* depicts the battle between Islam and Christianity in a nominally European location (Spain), it is the Holy Land that I shall address in this essay. Generally, my focus is restricted to films that depict peoples of the three major religions interacting with varying degrees of harmony and mayhem here. Although each of the three religions was born in conflict, the level of conflict intensified when those organized religions came into contact with each other in confined geographic environments—for example, Jerusalem. This is not to say that they have been in constant conflict, but rather that the conflict they have generated is both legendary and irresistible to filmmakers who recognize the inherent attraction of a fight. Conflict, in fact, is the hallmark of these films, for few spectacles are more intriguing, or horrifying, than religious zeal run amok.

Of the Old World desert films, those dealing with the Crusades provide an excellent opportunity to study how film portrays highly volatile religious issues and events. Rarely does religion operate outside of the larger sociopolitical framework, and so we might consider films about religious events to be depictions of how organized societies (the Egyptian caliphates; the Ottoman Empire; medieval Europe) interact with each other on matters of faith. Moreover, as in all films about intercultural dramas, these films are liable to reflect the personal political sentiments of their filmmakers. As we know from the works of Rosenstone and Toplin, among others, the historical film is rarely objective.[3] Its subjectivity works for and against the film, as is readily evident in films about the Crusades.

Although the Crusades began nearly a thousand years ago, their legacy is still visible in the Holy Land. Near Jerusalem, for example, one can still see remnants of the Crusaders' castles on rugged hillsides overlooking the Jordan Valley. The fabled Dead Sea and River Jordan shimmer in the middle ground, while the mountains of Judea and the Jordanian desert form the horizon. In the foreground are barren and chalky hills marked by the telltale tracks of cattle and sheep tended for millennia by Bedouins. Here the impressive ruins of stone towers punctuate the horizon. From the bases of these sentinels, remnants of walls meander across the rocky ridges like ramshackle versions of the Great Wall of China. These "Crusader castles" dot the entire landscape of Levant, including Palestine, Jordan, and Syria. Their ruins are reminders of the Crusaders' attempts to secure the area from the Muslims about a thousand years ago. They stand as a tangible reminder of an ongoing cultural divide, which has at times seemed more like a geological fault line. On one side of it, one experiences the presence of the *West,* as exemplified by the Crusades of the Middle Ages. On the other, the *East* is manifested in the Arab or Islamic presence in the landscape. In reality, of course, Israel and a few places of religious diversity are virtually surrounded by the largely Islamic Arab world, which stretches virtually unbroken about 3,000 miles westward across northern Africa and an equal distance eastward to Pakistan and western India. Although the largest number of Muslims live in Southeast Asia, we popularly associate Islam with the desert. As Muslim scholar M. A. Muqtedar Khan observes, "The Middle East exists on the borderlines, between modernity and tradition, between religion and politics, between East and West, independence and imperialism, between authenticity and uncritical emulation of the West."[4]

Just as the Middle East today is marked by great tensions between

Jews and Muslims, it was once a boundary between Christians and the peoples (Jews and Muslims) that they had briefly driven from Jerusalem during the Crusades. In this essay the provocative terms *Crusaders* and *Saracens* are used advisedly, with the understanding that labels are as incendiary and misleading as they are characteristic of particular times. By Crusaders, I mean practicing Christians who may be Catholics or Byzantine/Eastern Orthodox or (after the Reformation of 1517) Protestants. They may be Westerners from Europe or even the Americas. By Saracens, I mean not only nomadic peoples of Arabic heritage, as the term is used today, but—as the term was used by Europeans in the Middle Ages—any of the indigenous peoples of the Middle East who are Muslims. They may in fact be called by many names closely tied to their ethnic identity—Arabs, Turks, Bedouins, and so on. To Westerners, they are the Islamic "other."[5] Filmmakers portraying the Crusades also use the term *Saracens*—at least one of the aspects of the Middle Ages that they depict with some accuracy.

My main focus is on the portion of the region that was once called the Levant or Eastern Mediterranean, including parts of the Arabian peninsula and the Holy Land. This, of course, is near the epicenter of one of the most dramatic events in cultural history, the codification of religious law that led to the creation of Hebraic/Jewish culture and religion about 3,500 years ago. Christians trace the birth of their religion to Jerusalem (and nearby Nazareth and Bethlehem) about two thousand years ago. It was this locale that became an obsession for the Crusaders in the Middle Ages, who hoped to recapture the city of Jerusalem from "infidels" (Jews and Muslims). For their part, the Jews had a very early claim on the city, but through dispersals over the last two thousand years, they lost control of it to Muslims following the birth of that younger and very energetic religion—Islam—in about 615 A.D.

Lured by the desire to experience the desert and village locale where Christianity was founded, Christians began making long pilgrimages to the Holy Land as early as 250 A.D.[6] Some stayed there as ascetic monks, but others returned to Europe with inspirational stories. The number of pilgrims to the Holy Land increased substantially by 900 A.D. So, too, did tensions between returning Christians and indigenous peoples who were either Jews or Muslims. The destruction of the Church of the Holy Sepulchre in 1009, ordered by the Fatamid caliph Al-Hakim, is often cited as the catalyst for the Crusades against infidels. Although widely considered the act of a deranged caliph, this desecration was actually part of a pattern involving the destruction of Christian churches as tensions between "infidels" and Christians escalated. By 1070, the Seljukian Turks had captured Jerusalem, and other Christian cities in the region fell within the next two decades. By 1073, Pope Gregory VII considered military action to retake the entire area from the Turks—an idea acted on about twenty years later by his successor, Pope Urban II, in the 1090s. Historians widely interpret the Crusaders' actions to be as geopolitical as they were religious. By the 1090s, the Pope sought to solidify the power of the Roman Church in the face of increasing bickering and fragmentation in medieval Europe. This was a time when the church was split in two, with Constantinople and Rome representing its two faces. However, there is no doubt that religion fueled the Crusaders' passion as strongly as did the Pope's Machiavellian efforts to politically unify, and control, feuding European Christians. More recently, the Crusades have been interpreted as a method by which Europeans' self-realization occurred. Then, too, the religious zeal of the Crusaders in destroying the infidel may have been fueled by the militant Muslims who were overtaking Spain and moving into France, sometimes putting to death those who refused to adopt the Muslim faith.

Ultimately urged to action by Pope Urban II in 1097, the Crusaders fought their way into the Holy Land by way of Turkey. Their conquest of Jerusalem was undeniably bloody, their own accounts revealing that they killed every Jew and Muslim—man, woman, child—they encountered. By the early twelfth century, the Christians had retaken most of the area in what has been called the First Crusade. However, by the 1140s, European Christian domination in the region was threatened by lack of internal cohesion and increasing hostility by Muslim/Byzantine forces. Between 1144 and 1187, the Christian states in the Levant were destroyed. The Second Crusades (1145–47), conducted by Louis VII, sought to reverse the losses but ended in failure. The Third Crusade, led by Richard Coeur-de-Lion (Richard the Lion-Hearted) and Philip Augustus, was a four-year effort (1188–92) that has become *the* defining campaign, at least in popular culture. Although the Third Crusade was but one of many such episodes, it involves several highly visible and powerful leaders, including two in particular—King Richard and Saladin—who epitomize the kind of great men in conflict dramas that filmmakers find so irresistible. It also stands out as the most "literary" of the Crusades: As the subject of Sir Walter Scott's *The Talisman* (1825), the Third Crusade became the archetype for romantic intrigue and adventure acted out in an exotic, yet undoubtedly Christian, locale.

In the Fourth Crusade (1204), Constantinople fell to the Christians. The Fifth Crusade in 1217 witnessed the fall of Damietta to the Christians, and about a decade later the Sixth Crusade began (1228–29), ending a decade later (1239). St. Louis led the Seventh (1249–52) and Eighth (1270) Crusades. By 1291, the Crusades essentially ended as the Christians lost control of Syria and the Kingdom of Jerusalem.[7] Collectively, the Crusades left a lasting impact on the Middle East. A scholar of the region observes that "the Crusades, in my opinion, constitute the beginning of the First World War in human history, and it was initiated to realize the meaning of religious identity."[8]

In retrospect, the Crusades failed to achieve the Christians' goal of routing infidels from the Holy Land. Despite their attempt to carve the region into Christian European fiefdoms, the Crusaders could not establish a lasting presence. But instead of giving up, they simply changed their strategy. Although some Christians persisted in claiming portions of the region, their efforts after around 1300 turned toward missionizing instead of military solutions. Rather than dominating, the Christians now found themselves able, if not content, to become a tolerated minority in many areas, with hopes of ultimately converting (rather than massacring) the infidels. For its part, Islam had a long history of conversion (or death) at sword point but also actively converted peoples peacefully. That more peaceful activity, however, tends to make less dramatic films than the violence we have come to expect in literature and movies.

ORIENTALISM

The Crusades, while very complex, can ultimately be seen as bringing the West face to face with the Eastern other (that is, other lands and peoples) on repeated occasions. The legacy endures as the word *crusade* itself, and though it has been broadened to mean any zealous fight to rectify a wrong, it is decidedly inflammatory to Muslims in the region. One recalls the outrage expressed by the Muslim world when U.S. President George W. Bush called the war on terror a "crusade." Of course Bush did not use the word crusade to mean an all-out war against all Muslims, but the word itself is so loaded that it was interpreted as such. Interestingly, the word *crusade* became negative not a thousand years ago but more recently when the Arab world became conscious of the growing power of the West in the last two centuries.[9] In the West, the term evokes a galvanic response as a reference to something worth fighting for, while in the East it provides a cause to fight against a threat from outside the region. Those who believe that *crusade* means a war against Islam should recall that certain fighter-bomber airplanes during the Cold War bore the name "Crusader" when in fact they were intended to humble Communists, not Muslims.

That the word *crusade* means different things in the West and East goes to the heart of this essay. It is here that I would like to discuss the term *Orient* in more detail. By *Orient* I mean both a *place* (the East) and an *idea* (the supposed character of the East). Such a discussion can never be separated from the concept of Orientalism—the Western fascination with the East (both the place and the idea). The term *Orientalism* dates from the late 1700s, when it meant the study, even appreciation, of the East or Orient. But as we have seen, Orientalism can be traced to the Middle Ages, during which the East was also considered tangible and very different from Christendom. Actually, the fascination with the East is venerable, dating at least to the time of Alexander the Great (356–323 B.C.).

Edward Said wrote that "the Orient was almost a European invention, and had been since antiquity a place of romance, exotic beings, haunting memories and landscapes, [and] remarkable experiences"—that now form part of a colonial discourse with the Eastern world.[10] Three nations in particular—England, France, and the United States—have succumbed to this discourse and the spell of Orientalism. Orientalism above all essentializes (that is, overly simplifies) what is in reality a very complex part of the world. It can do so in many ways. In "Gender and Culture of Empire," Ella Shohat astutely notes that Orientalism exoticizes and eroticizes the East on male terms, its women often portrayed in terms of rape and polygamy.[11] Gaylyn Studlar explores the theme from a different perspective, arguing that interpretations of varied dance routines presented the major stereotypes of women as vamps, Cleopatras, and Salomes. Matthew Bernstein observes that it was "the self-assertive, exhibitionist 'orientalized female' who temporarily blurred the boundaries of gender, ethnicity, and race."[12] For her part, the Oriental woman has considerable power over the hapless male, usually but not always a Westerner who inevitably falls under her spell. In promoting the 1922 Austrian-Hungarian film *Sodom and Gomorrha: The Legend of Sin and Punishment*, the publicists claimed that the actress who played both the Queen of Syria and Lot's wife was "a sphinx with mystical eyes, a girl who evokes one's wildest desires and craves sacrifice, so that an honest man, robbed of his wits, is driven to commit deeds beyond his better judgment."[13] Cinematically speaking, filmmakers find it difficult to resist such a seductress who can heat up a plot and draw audiences in search of vicarious pleasure.

Geographically speaking, the Orient is very difficult to define, for it literally means any place east of the West. Typically, we speak of two Easts—the far East and the near East. They are both exotic, which is to say different enough from the West to be as easily understood intuitively as they are hard to define geographically. For their part, geographers have long considered "the East" too simplistic and divided it into many subregions—Southeast Asia, Indonesia, the Middle East, and so on. These subregions may be based on physical geography but are normally cultural. Then, too, historians and social critics may define the East as areas where fundamentally different religions and cultures—for example, Islam or Buddhism—dominate. It is interesting that literary critics and writers themselves offer noteworthy definitions of Orientalism that are based less on geography than on *a state of mind*. For example, Argentine poet and essayist Jorge Luis Borges stated that there "is something we feel as the Orient . . . but . . . I don't know how I can define it." Borges, however, went on to define the Orient as well as anyone ever has: "It is above all a world of extremes in which people are very happy or very unhappy, very rich or very poor. A world of Kings who do not explain what they do. Of Kings who are, we might say, as irresponsible as Gods."[14] We recognize this Orient even today as a place where a despot like Saddam Hussein could increase the number of his presidential palaces from nine (in 1990) to sixty-five (in 2003) while his people endured the grinding poverty imposed by war sanctions that he consistently ignored. As historians Ian Buruma and Avishai Margalit so aptly put it, "Saddam Hussein, for one, liked to portray himself as Saladin, savior of the Arabs, riding his white steed to wipe out the infidels."[15] It is no coincidence that Hussein was obsessed with writing novels, for despots themselves are often self-consciously aware of their power and fixated on their legacy. Timothy Weiss summed up Borges' understanding of the Orient as "having the shape of a story; in this story-within-stories, one eventually finds, he surmises, one's own tale and destiny."[16]

I like this definition of the Orient as a story-within-a-story in which one finds one's own tale and destiny. It not only incorporates a touch of Arabian intertextuality but also may help explain the nearly insatiable Western interest in the East from ancient, and certainly Christian, times to the present. A despotic ruler playing God is conceivable in this place we have relegated to the exotic "other" because we believe that it is a place that has objectively different rules than those rules by which Western society normally plays: such an Orient is conceivable, and readily conceived, by Westerners as a place that serves as a counterpoint to ours. Just as we have persistently relegated the Orient to the exotic other, we have also remanded its peoples to the status of others. The concept of one's tale and destiny being a part of this story has had, and continues to have, a strong appeal to the Western mind. I might add that the reverse has also happened: the East also has a mind-set about the West, as potential intruder, that resonates to the present. That, of course, is Occidentalism, which although not discussed in this essay, is a topic receiving serious study.[17]

Although Edward Said branded Orientalism a phenomenon of late eighteenth- and early nineteenth-century imperialism, he recognized its earlier roots. Orientalism certainly personifies attitudes toward the East as early as in medieval times. The Crusades, in fact, may be seen as the precursor of institutionalized imperial authority (the Pope) orchestrating a political agenda toward the East. That East in this case was Jerusalem and the adjacent Holy Land as the threatened hearth of Christianity, and its occupiers—the Saracens—symbolized the despotism, barbarism, and exoticism that both repelled and lured the European mind. The Crusaders had no doubt that they had a rightful claim to the Holy Land, in part because their history could be traced there. The point is that the Middle East not only fascinates as the exotic but also lures as *the ultimate source* of our own Western culture. That points to an irony of modern times, as when American troops captured the mysterious, barbarically ruled city of Baghdad, which was simultaneously characterized as the birthplace of civilization and the site of extreme cruelty. This, some said, was a continuation of the Crusades—the West's ongoing desire to right barbaric wrongs in the East.

Much has been written on the original Crusades, but relatively little of it considers the strong element of Orientalism that they embody. Suffice it to say that medieval illustrated manuscripts like the *Marvels of the East* depict both places and their inhabitants as strange and threatening. This may at first seem surprising—after all, the Crusades supposedly involved Christians retaking the Holy Land as a place in which their faith (and their religious leader, Jesus) was born. However, that same Christianity portrays the place and its inhabitants as perennially corrupt and corruptible without intervention by its message of redemption. This is another way of saying that just as the concept of original sin casts the corporeal birthplace of the *soul* as hopelessly without purification by faith, so does it stipulate that the *land* of its religious birth requires purification—at times either by faith or by sword.

It is this passionate, even dangerous, belief that this essay addresses. My premise is that Orientalism first provides us the exotic other complete with excesses (of flesh, wealth, hubris) as a foil against which moral crusaders have reacted for at least 2,000 years. Orientalism is deeply entrenched, chronologically and spiritually, because it is an essential element in the binary thought system—light vs. dark, good vs. evil, saved vs. damned—that underlies Christianity (and, for that matter, Judaism and Islam). The inevitability of Orientalism in Western thought is also geographical. The Orient as East signifies two things. The first, lofty spiritualism, is associated with the rising of the sun in the east—hence the concept of Jerusalem at the *top* of early maps. Its lofty position there symbolizes that city's importance, and it persists in our using the word "orientation" to signify up (or top) on a map—even though that position is now conventionally north! But consider this: before that sun rose in the east, that was the very region from which darkness had to be replaced. Just as we might seek the sun by traveling west as a way of finding constant renewal, by looking eastward we find more than the rising sun: we also inevitably find the darkness that must be banished by the light. This, coupled with the fact that traveling eastward brought Europeans face to face with new (or rediscovered) environments like the desert—with its binary challenges as wilderness of temptation and nurturer of God's spirit through light[18]—made the East a place of great ambivalence. It also made the East greatly desired as a place where one's spiritual mettle could be tested.

Building on the general definition of Orientalism as a fascination with the East (and Easterners), I will next outline numerous traits associated with it. Some, admittedly, are not particularly politically correct, while others are uncritically flattering. Most, interestingly, are contradictory:

Wisdom. One of the most enduring beliefs about the Orient (and Orientals) is that it possesses a rich tradition of knowledge and learning. Much of this learning is philosophical, although science and technology are also present as either practical or arcane knowledge.

Ignorance. Simultaneously, the Orient is said to be a land of superstition, the masses of its people poorly educated and resistant to new ideas.

Sensuality. Another enduring aspect of the East is that it embodies the promise of earthly/sexual delights.

Asceticism. Simultaneously, the Orient is associated with a long tradition of self-denial both in the physical sense (fasting, abstinence) and intellectual sense (rejection of materialism).

Militancy. The concept of warfare as a way of life has long been associated with the Orient. Warlords, samurai, and armed bands abound geographically and chronologically: if periods of peace exist, they are unusual and inevitably ended by longer periods of violence.

Pacifism. Some peoples of the East, namely Buddhists and early Christians, astound us with their resistance to harming others.

Barbarism. In addition to more or less organized military action, the East is associated with extreme cruelty—torture, mutilation, assassination—that affects the civilian population in ways that terrify, and sometimes outrage, "civilized" peoples.

Meekness. Parts of the region possess peoples who are shy or taciturn—mysteriously silent and passive.

Duplicity. If, in the West, a man's value is determined by his ability to keep to his word, a popular stereotype about the Middle East

RICHARD FRANCAVIGLIA

is that falsehood and manipulation trump truth for both immediate and long-term ends.

Honesty. As if to mock the concept of duplicity, some people in the East pride themselves on being honorable, their word sealing any agreement.

Opulence. The palaces, treasures, and pomp of Eastern potentates are legendary. Normally, wealth is highly concentrated and prominently displayed.

Poverty. As if to counterbalance, even mock, opulence, there is the persistent, grinding poverty under which the masses of people live.

Regardless of how we may characterize these contrasting traits, the one that brands the region—and has no trait against which it can be contrasted—is its sense of *resignation*. Whereas the West is said to be obsessed with change, progress, and improvement, the East is invariably associated with endemic resignation—likely a consequence of the belief that irrepressible forces, or an irrepressible force called "fate," makes individual actions irrelevant. We see this time and again in literature and film, and I suspect it is because Christianity emphasizes the individual's role in implementing change for the better while a stereotypical view of Islam suggests that fate controls one's destiny.

If, as I have suggested, Orientalism is still operating in Western culture, what better way to seek its presence than in that most informative and misinformative medium of the last century—film. As historians, moreover, we are provided a wonderful opportunity to seek Orientalism in *any* type of film (for example, in two wildly different Arnold Schwarzenegger action films, *Conan the Barbarian* and *True Lies*). But even films we might not normally associate with the Crusades may be based on that type of Crusaders' quest. Consider, for a moment, *The Lord of the Rings* trilogy. Based on Tolkien's epic novel (first published in 1954), this three-part film adventure features hapless hobbits leaving their comfortable green land to venture southeastward to the arid, mountainous land of Mordor, where evil reigns. In order to restore peace to the world, the hobbits must reunite a ring with its original source of power. Sound familiar? It should, because this grail-like quest is overtly spiritual. In the hands of the filmmakers, *The Lord of the Rings* reveals the Orientalism built into the concept of journeying east to restore monumental imbalances. The monstrous armies encountered there sport southwestern Asian armor and are aided by huge, elephant-like creatures. If this is not suggestive enough of the Orient, the film's superb musical score by Howard Shore elaborates. It features a stunning contrast between the lilting Gaelic music of home—Christianized in places with soaring cathedral-like choruses that reveal the contrast between good and evil—and the much darker scoring of the East's evil opposition. The latter resonates with clashing gongs and cymbals and a dizzying pace reminiscent of saber dances, and features romantic refrains reminiscent of the *Arabian Nights*.

This essay, however, analyzes several historically themed films that treat the actual Crusades to decipher persistent conceptions and misconceptions. To do so, I go beyond Edward Said's informative but ultimately politically-charged definition of Orientalism. Whereas Said considers Orientalism to be imperialistic, racist, and ethnocentric,[19] I concur with Timothy Weiss that Orientalism is so important and so richly textured that it would be unfortunate to politicize it instead of recognizing its deeper emotional and even transformative qualities.[20]

Orientalism in this more perceptual sense can actually *reverse* Western perspectives—that is, it can literally reorient (pun intended) the observer. In his insightful anthropological investigation into the film *Lawrence of Arabia,* Steven C. Caton posed the question succinctly enough: "The problem is this: how does one get to an intellectually adequate criticism of such artistically complex and ideologically loaded works?" Caton observes that criticism and interpretation must take several factors into account, including the realization that dominant institutions can no longer be seen as monolithic or uniform and that "the difference between center and margin, between dominant groups and subalterns, is not as stark as may have once been supposed; that, in fact, a subtle yet complex collaboration has historically existed between the two." Caton further notes that "the center" may actually produce works that are "critical of the hegemonic project they propose and of those individuals who perpetuate it." He calls his approach the "dialectical critique."[21] In this case, the Orient can be geographically and psychologically *inside* and *outside*—the *inside* being a movement toward transformation and a deepening appreciation of the other(s), while the *outside* signifies a movement away from modernity toward the development of a sensibility to a mythical and narrative appreciation of the past that had been occluded or erased.[22] Orientalism, in other words, serves to both conserve and subvert.[23]

Although Orientalism in film has a long history, I would like to begin by discussing one aspect—sexuality—in the film discussed in the introduction to this essay. In one pivotal early scene in *The Conqueror,* Wayne/ Khan plans to raid a camp and abduct Bortai, the Tartar princess played by Susan Hayward. When his brother warns him that this is not wise, that he should follow his mind rather than his passions, Wayne replies, "My blood says I must have the Tartar woman." Although more humor-

RICHARD FRANCAVIGLIA

ous than realistic, this line from *The Conqueror* reminds us how hard put writers can be to know exactly what someone from another culture and another time may have said. Wayne's lines in *The Conqueror*, classics in film camp, play—however clumsily—to the theme of Mongol as sexual predator and to the Oriental woman as sexual object. In *The Conqueror*, the sexuality is directed at a royal woman who is lighter complected than the Mongols but still nominally Oriental. When that sexual energy involves people from two different cultures, it introduces the element of the exotic into the equation, which is what Orientalism is about on a very visceral level. The equation has two components: the attractiveness of the beautiful, exotic Oriental woman and the fear of the powerful, sexually potent Oriental male who would defile the whiter woman.

In his critical interpretation of Hollywood films about Arabs, Jack Shaheen identifies a number of stereotypes that "inherited and embellished Europe's pre-existing Arab caricatures" and he further asserts that "almost *all* Hollywood depictions of Arabs are *bad* ones."[24] The stereotypes:

Cast Arabs as villains and/or buffoons;
Depict sheikhs as unattractive and rapacious;
Humiliate, demonize, and eroticize Arab women.

Moreover, these films are not monolithic but provide separate sets of stereotypes linked to country of origin. For example, they portray Egypt in terms of mummies, beggars, and souk swindlers, while Palestinians are most often cast as terrorists. Shaheen's point is that most Arabs are none of the above, but instead are a diverse people engaged in all manner of work. There is no doubt that these stereotypes exist, but how do they play out in historically themed films about the Middle East? In this sense, the tumultuous period of the Crusades presents an opportunity to compare the historical record with films depicting an important event that brought Europeans and Middle Easterners face to face in a set of battles in the field and ultimately on-screen.

THE CRUSADES ON FILM

We commonly associate the East with sensuality, but it is also associated with religion—especially the birth of Judeo-Christian religion and later threats to Christianity by non-Christians. Consider that subgenre of military films, those about the Crusades. As early as 1903, *A Tale of the Crusades* dramatized the event, followed by *The Crusaders* in 1911. The knights in these silent films[25] battled the forces of evil to reclaim the Holy

Land. Cecil B. DeMille's *The Crusades* (1935) represents the "costume picture," that is, one that required elaborate costumes to portray the feel of the historic era depicted. *The Crusades* was produced when films were introduced by a written text that appeared on screen. The film begins with a view of a small desert city that the titling claims is "JERUSALEM— Through the ages the city sacred to men." This declaration underscores the ecumenical aspects of the city sacred to Jews, Christians, and Muslims. The action in *The Crusades* begins in 1187 A.D., when the "Saracens" take the city, and women are sold into slavery. The opening scenes horrify and titillate. The Saracen slave trader displays shackled women like so much livestock being driven to the sexual slaughterhouse. For their part, the Christian women are angelic and stoic—clinging to their crucifixes as the Saracens tear them from their sisters. These scenes incite and infuriate. They are charged with sexual energy and plumb deeply held sexual anxieties wherein the savage barbarians not only dominate women but also defile them at will.

Equally revealing, and closely related, is the reference to the senseless destruction of the Holy Sepulchre and other Christian sites in Jerusalem by Al-Hakim, the Fatamid caliph of Egypt. In DeMille's *The Crusades*, a zealous Christian hermit confronts the brilliant Islamic leader Saladin almost two centuries after Al-Hakim's barbaric act, but the memory of this desecration evidently still resonates. So, too, does the frequent

The Christian Hermit urges holy war (from The Crusades, *Paramount, 1935; courtesy Photofest)*

RICHARD FRANCAVIGLIA

molestation of Christian pilgrims bound for Jerusalem. Saladin is the Muslim leader closely associated with the Crusades—notably the Third Crusade. In DeMille's film, Saladin is also called the "Sultan of Islam," and in that role he epitomizes the wise but ruthless potentate: swarthy, intelligent, dangerous, charismatic. The hermit—probably patterned after Peter the Hermit, who was involved in the First Crusade—symbolizes the obsessed religious zealot. The hermit warns Saladin that he will go to Europe and return with knights who will set things straight. The next scene shows the hermit in England, issuing a call to arms. He urges all Christians to retake "the Holy Land, to free the Tomb of our Lord."

The Crusaders are soon united and make their way to the port of Acre, where the hermit proclaims a warning: "Oh, Infidels, the Crusade has crossed the sea." When Saladin arrives to defend Acre, the Crusaders declare war. In the midst of this warfare, a special effort is made to protect King Richard's wife, Berengaria, "from the Infidel"—a reference that foretells Saladin's romantic interest in her. When Berengaria is shot by Saladin's men, the increasingly protective Saladin claims that "Allah has sent her to me: I will not let her die." Saladin is clearly smitten with Berengaria, telling her, "You have crept into my heart." Saladin wants to marry Berengaria, claiming that she is no longer the wife of the Lion King because "Islam does not accept a Christian marriage." Moreover, Saladin fatalistically tells Berengaria, "It is *written* that you should come to me." This fatalism is one of the most perplexing, and even disturbing, elements of Orientalism to Christians, who generally believe in free will and personal responsibility. For her part, Berengaria is cast as a selfless and strong woman who exhibits Christian traits. To save her husband Richard's life and end the violent Crusades, she will give herself to Saladin. This willingness to sacrifice places her in the role of a martyr and Saladin in the role of irresistible villain.

The drama of the Crusaders' attack on Acre is portrayed as the Crusaders' entrance into the Holy Land. As one might expect of a DeMille epic, the battle scenes are spectacular. So, too, is the political intrigue that is depicted in abundance. Not only are the Crusaders shown as factionally betraying each other, as they did, but the movie also focuses on the importance of honor—man-to-man honor, as Richard and Saladin dramatically interact on several occasions. Here DeMille softens his criticism of Saladin. As the action continues, Richard and Saladin form the type of bond that only great leaders can: when Richard comes to Saladin's tent, the Muslim leader proclaims, "By Allah, I wish you were my brother, not my foe." Richard finally sees the error of his ways: violence is not the answer to reestablishing a Christian presence in Jerusalem. Saladin's magnanimity is profound—he graciously enables Richard and

The Crusaders march in Jerusalem (from The Crusades, *Paramount, 1935; courtesy Photofest)*

Berengaria to reunite and to enter the Holy City, where Berengaria places the sword on the tomb as a symbol that violence is renounced.

DeMille's *The Crusades* is an interesting and complex film. Although it justifies the militarism of the Crusaders in their desire to retake Jerusalem, it shows how Saladin's wisdom led to peace rather than continued mayhem. *The Crusades* also portrays the duplicitous nature of two crusading factions—nominally, the French versus the English—which helped undermine the Crusades. Moreover, it portrays the internecine deviousness in Richard's own family as his brother schemes to kill him and take the throne of Jerusalem. A close examination of this film reveals why pro-Arab sources such as Jack G. Shaheen's *Reel Bad Arabs* are simplistic. Shaheen says *The Crusades* casts Arabs as "VILLAINS," but he is oversimplifying. Although, as Shaheen notes, the Crusaders' villainy toward Arabs is downplayed, *The Crusades* reveals that Saladin and his men are ultimately more trustworthy than many of Richard's countrymen. This is DeMille at his most subversive, depicting Saracens as morally superior to the Crusaders.

Released during the Great Depression, *The Crusades* has a message of unification against overwhelming odds. To audiences, the film's message must have resonated as one of hope. In *The Crusades*, Saladin is portrayed in classic Orientalist fashion, as both manipulative and wise; yet, he is ultimately a man who yields to the power of God/Allah and is basically honorable. Played by Anglo-American actor Ian Keith, Saladin is stereotyped as swarthy and intense, with expressive eyes that suggest both mischief and intelligence. For his part, Richard is brave, headstrong, and naïve. In *The Crusades*, it is Richard, as a surrogate for the Anglo-American male, who learns painful lessons in sacrifice and humility. Given the potential for *The Crusades* to treat Saladin as subhuman, especially in light of DeMille's Christian zeal, this Arab leader's relatively positive depiction is noteworthy. True, Saladin is stereotyped and his motives and personality criticized, but that is one of the inevitable characteristics of films about peoples from other cultures and times. The remarkable thing about Saladin in DeMille's film is that he is ultimately wise—far wiser than King Richard.

As filming was just beginning on *The Crusades*, DeMille met with several major executives and the screenwriter. A transcript of that conversation between DeMille and Paramount executive Barney Glazer reveals how sensitive a studio can be about the "political" impact of depicting history on-screen:

BARNEY GLAZER: Will we get in trouble with England and the English colonies for your suggestion that Berengaria, queen—or near queen, was desired of and spent some time in the tent of Saladin? It is a daring invention.

CECIL B. DEMILLE: I would think not. Even in England they thought Berengaria was a steamship until we started the picture. [Even] I did not know it until I read Harold Lamb's book.

Harold Lamb was the author and screenwriter whose book inspired the film project. Lamb responded that Berengaria was something of a mystery: "As a matter of fact," he added, "we know nothing about her except where she came from, where she was crowned and where she was married to Richard, and [that] she appeared to the Pope in Rome—but everything else in her history is a blank. . . . On her return after his [Richard's] death, she just disappeared."

That made Berengaria the perfect character for a historically themed film based, in part, on the historical record and in part on the historical novel. The studio's concern about possible *English* reactions is interesting. However, even more interesting during that conversation is the evident absence of any concern about the possible *Arab* response. *The Crusades*, of course, was made for English-speaking audiences and produced from an Anglo-American perspective. In 1935, Arab audiences were not anticipated, so the question would not have been asked. For his part, DeMille defended the script against some strong concern by studio executives at that meeting. He observed that "a character like Richard, who is the audience" will be able to "show his acquirement [sic] of God and spiritual understanding and let the audience take it from that." When asked about the contradictory role of Saladin, who is both a supporter of "desecrations" and "a world-wide hero," DeMille responded that "Saladin comes along with his attitude to make the audience feel the Crusade—to make them want to get up and fight." Paramount executive E. Lloyd Sheldon confirmed that what DeMille called "that spiritual thing" was paramount in this film. Sheldon added, "It is awfully important. . . . The danger may be that [by complicating the plot] you have lost the Crusades feeling. . . . You think of these wretched souls that went over there and went through privations, when actually the Kings were only thinking of [acquiring] another province." DeMille agreed that losing the "Crusades feeling," as Sheldon called it, "would be fatal." [26] Ironically, although *The Crusades* ultimately lost money for the studio, its relatively heroic treatment of Saladin paid off in terms of DeMille's conscience. DeMille stated twenty-five years later in his autobiography: "Thanks to our treatment of the subject and the wonderfully sensitive performance of Ian Keith as Saladin, *The Crusades* has been one of my most popular pictures in the Middle East." [27]

King Richard and the Crusaders

About two decades after *The Crusades*, Hollywood released *King Richard and the Crusaders* (1954). Like its earlier counterpart, *King Richard and the Crusaders* was inspired by Sir Walter Scott's novel *The Talisman*, which became a best seller upon its publication in 1825. This 1954 film plays heavily on the Scottish-English tension that is so palpable in Scott's novel. King Richard is vexed by a Scotsman named Kenneth who, like all stereotyped Scots, is insolent and brave. Richard mistrusts the Scot but senses that he is honorable. Directed by David Butler, *King Richard and the Crusaders* was a box office hit that perpetuated a number of stereotypes—positive and negative—about Arabs (and, for that matter, Scots). As with most historically themed Crusader films, the drama is nominally religious and political but also centers on a romantic triangle. This time, however, it is Edith, King Richard's beautiful blonde cousin, who is at the center, while Saladin and Kenneth the Scot vie for her hand in marriage. Richard, of course, opposes his cousin even considering marrying a Scot, much less being courted by a Saracen. Moreover, Richard is constantly in danger from Crusaders from other nations and even from his own Britain. In conspiring to assassinate Richard and rule Jerusalem, a despicable countryman states that "I've always fancied the Oriental mode of living." Does Orientalism get any more explicit—and decadent—than this?

In *King Richard and the Crusaders*, it is Saladin, played by Rex Harrison, who is both wise *and* honorable. The West has long been fascinated by Islam's authorization of polygamy, and Saladin is said to have many wives—a fact that reveals the sexually dominant undercurrent in Orientalism. King Richard, played by George Sanders, is ambivalent about Saladin, who disguises himself as a doctor to heal Richard's near fatal wound inflicted by duplicitous Crusaders. When Richard criticizes Saladin, Edith reminds Richard that he himself has often said that "Saladin is a man of chivalry." Saladin is also brimming with sexual energy and passion—the classic characteristics of an Oriental potentate. With a telling metaphor, Richard later says of Saladin's interest in Edith—"he knows the geography of the female like the palm of his hand." But Saladin is, in the Orientalist tradition, ultimately wise and able to resist temptation. Although Saladin is smitten by Edith and engineers her removal from the British Crusaders, he ultimately gives her up, stating that it is "a good man who learns what is not his" to take.

In *King Richard and the Crusaders*, Edith is at the center of a political drama. She is not only beautiful but also idealistic and principled—a subtle feminized symbol of Christ the Peacemaker. Saladin is not only captivated by Edith's charms but also attracted to her independence and

King Richard and the Crusaders *(Warner Bros., 1954; courtesy Photofest)*

her strong personality (which, he acknowledges, is stronger than that of a "Moslem woman"). In this film, Saladin is the consummate geopolitical thinker who realizes that marrying "the Nazarene" Edith will not only give him everything he desires in a woman but also will help him extend his power into Europe. Doing so, however, would necessitate Saladin giving up his religion for Edith, which he is unable to do. For her part, Edith is so tired of the Crusaders' fighting that she envisions that marrying Saladin would enable her to "bring peace to the East." In *King Richard and the Crusaders,* Saladin is ultimately selfless and recognizes that he is *destined* to give up Edith. He concludes that "I have learned so much. I have learned that I am a Saracen—completely and forever."

Saladin

Although it is difficult to compare how films from different eras treat essentially the same event, I would like to next discuss how the Arabic world views the Crusades cinematically—albeit nearly thirty years after DeMille's film and a decade after David Butler's 1954 film. The film *Saladin* (1963), available only from Arab Films, provides an interesting counterpoint to the American films discussed above. *Saladin* begins with Arabs being routed from Jerusalem by the Crusaders and suggests that this defeat inspired Saladin to unite the Arabs. As one might expect, this film depicts the Christian Crusaders as treacherous and craven. They are shown first stealing from unarmed Arab pilgrims and then massacring them. Despite this bloodletting, a Crusader appears insatiable, yelling "Nothing will quench my thirst but Saladin's blood." The Arabs in this film are, to a man, honorable. One of them, a man smitten by the beauty of a Crusader woman, spares her life; in return, she shoots him with an arrow. Nevertheless, love blossoms amid war, as it does in virtually all historically themed epics. The symbolism here is clear: betrayal awaits one who sympathizes with the Crusaders, who are shown as selfish, even insane. However, one can still love one's enemy—either selflessly or romantically. That, too, appears to be "written."

Continuing with the theme of the Crusaders' depravity, *Saladin* depicts the French Crusader Renaud as both insane *and* cowardly. In one telling scene that Arabs, as desert dwellers, would find especially abhorrent, Renaud secretly drinks water meant for his thirsty troops—and then denies it when accused. For his part, Saladin claims that he only wants "equality for Christians and Muslims." As if possessing considerable insight about Orientalism in the Middle Ages, a Crusader back in Europe observes that "all the treasures of the East have been seized by Saladin." Less than a minute later, in a scene that takes place in Jerusa-

(L.) Ahmed Mazhar as Saladin (from Saladin, *Arab Films, 1963)*

lem, Saladin observes of the Crusaders that "the magic of the East seems to have bewitched them." Both these references to the East, as well as others in the film, are of course from hindsight in the 1960s. Moreover, they seem self-consciously Orientalist from an Arab perspective—that is, the Arab scriptwriters and filmmakers know the historic allure of the East to Europeans. This is Occidentalism, and it reveals the Easterners' fascination and obsession with, and essentializing of, the West.

In this Occidentalism, virtually all Westerners are morally bankrupt materialists. Brave, handsome, and astute, Saladin is well aware of the Crusaders' moral bankruptcy: when the Crusaders betray each other, Saladin is not only disgusted but actually disappointed. In trying to make peace with King Richard, he is betrayed at every turn. "How . . ." Saladin asks, "can you trust a man who betrays his own cause?" When Saladin comes to help the wounded King Richard, he serves in the noble role of a doctor operating under a self-imposed truce. This reveals some of the complexity of the real Saladin, who is by turns heroic, intelligent, wise, and a peacemaker—never a duplicitous villain. Richard's wife senses both the greatness of Saladin and his people—and the corruptness of hers. When recounting a horrendous act, she observes that "Arabs would not commit such a crime." The fact that a Christian woman recognizes the Crusaders' depravity makes them all the more pathetic— and the woman potentially reclaimable as a Muslim upon conversion.

In defending the city of Jerusalem, which the subtitles identify as "the city of the Living God," Saladin literally has Allah on his side. His skills as a diplomat and spiritual leader are evident by the film's finale, when peace is finally restored. In a scene that appears strangely European, Richard and Saladin reach the accord as "Adeste Fideles" ("O Come All Ye Faithful") is sung and a soft snow falls on Jerusalem—on Christmas Eve! Snow does fall on Jerusalem from time to time, but its occurrence on Christmas seems calculated to appeal to European and American Christians. Moreover, the accord between the Crusaders and Arabs suggests the spirit of Saladin's tolerance toward other religions. Yet the message of Islam's control of this geographic location is apparent. "Thank you, Allah," Saladin says, "by your will, you have made your servant victorious."

Like all popular films, *Saladin* endorses cultural values. As in *The Crusades* and *King Richard and the Crusaders,* the film *Saladin* is as propagandistic as it is artistic. In offering a relatively simple black-and-white portrayal of a very complex situation, it omits mention of several misdeeds in the treatment of Christians that, in part, precipitated the Crusades. By emphasizing the widely lauded leadership of Saladin, it avoids any ambiguity on the Arab side. The film *Saladin* is overtly political in that it builds on the self-consciously Occidentalist theme that Westerners/Christians are doomed to succumb to the lure of the East. Considering the time in which it was produced, the film *Saladin* served to unify Islam and Christianity against threats from outside as Israel gained strength after being established by the United Nations fifteen years earlier.

Like the American films *The Crusades* and *King Richard and the Crusaders,* the Arab film *Saladin* relies on stereotypes. The actor portraying King Richard in *Saladin* is oddly made up, his skin appearing clay-like as his makeup obviously attempts to disguise a different, perhaps swarthier, complexion. Moreover, Richard's red beard appears unconvincing. One can excuse this because these are Arab actors playing Europeans, but that is not surprising. Until relatively recently, American films also used white actors to play all manner of ethnic people—Native Americans, Asians, and Arabs. Rex Harrison as Saladin in *King Richard and the Crusaders* is a case in point.

The Kingdom of Heaven

The most recent Crusader film—*Kingdom of Heaven* (2005)—was released during a time of heightened conflict between the West and the Arab world. A year and a half before its release, on the second anniversary of September 11, while the film was still in production, National

Public Radio's *All Things Considered* conducted a remarkable interview with the film's director, Ridley Scott. Given the increased scrutiny that historic films were receiving and the tensions following September 11, NPR and listeners calling in asked Scott some penetrating questions about his philosophy of portraying history on film. As if anticipating criticism concerning the historical accuracy of *Kingdom of Heaven*, Scott admitted that "story books are what we base our movies on, and what we base our characters on."[28]

And yet Scott went on to note that all of the main characters in *Kingdom of Heaven* were based on real people associated with the Crusades. As with other earlier films about the Crusades, to which *Kingdom of Heaven* is an homage, Scott's film begins with written words on the screen that set the scene in medieval times, notably medieval France. The film's plot focuses on Balian (Orlando Bloom), a French blacksmith who joins his father (Liam Neeson) on a crusade in 1184. That date is important, for it is shortly *before* the Third Crusade began. In a sense, *Kingdom of Heaven* is a revealing prequel to the Third Crusade and all other films about it. Over the next decade after his arrival in Jerusalem, Balian becomes the Crusade's principal knight. As one might imagine, this positions Balian to become part of the tumultuous action leading to the Third Crusade. Balian's sojourn in the vicinity of Kerak (Syria) and Jerusalem gives him ample opportunity to observe the fanaticism of the Knights Templar, better understand the Muslim religion, and—predictably—fall in love with Sibylla (Eva Green), the beautiful sister of the Leper King Baldwin IV and wife of a Crusader opportunist.

In *Kingdom of Heaven*, Sibylla is the perfect trope for the exoticized Eastern woman. Although a Christian and actually a Westerner, her ornate clothing and veil provide an aura of mystery. Sibylla effectively becomes transcultural, in a manner of speaking—a Middle Eastern–styled woman who adopts a dual personality—veiled in public while sensual in private. As her early interest in Balian emerges, she tells him that "in the East, between one person and another, there is only light." This symbolically self-conscious line is not really "Eastern" at all, but classically Western—the reference to light referring to dawn as well as to enlightenment. This line is all the more ironic when Sibylla blows out the only candle in the room, literally throwing Balian into darkness and then throwing herself upon him. This, of course, is the East at its most seductive—physically tempting and intellectually enigmatic. Sibylla's mention of the word "East" and her depiction as a seductress in such a recent film serves as a reminder that ero-Orientalism is still very much alive in the twenty-first century.

As in all films depicting this period during the Crusades, Saladin looms large as brave, shrewd, wise, and compassionate. Played by veteran Syrian actor Ghassan Massoud, Saladin is the consummate Arab leader—swarthy, bearded, powerful, and philosophical/spiritual. In *Kingdom of Heaven,* we are treated to a first in Western film history: Saladin's name is pronounced properly (Sah-lah-hah-Déen) rather than as a word sounding similar to the popular American way Aladdin is pronounced (Sah-lah-dinh). *Kingdom of Heaven* was criticized for its political correctness, and there is some validity to that criticism as it appears to be the first Western film to make absolutely no reference to the destruction of the Holy Sepulchre. Another criticism was that Scott's film seemed to miss capturing the religious zeal (rather than the political motivation) of the Crusaders. That said, *Kingdom of Heaven* is still the most nuanced of the Crusader films.

Like all films about the Crusades, *Kingdom of Heaven* refers to Islamic fatalism as characters observe that "Allah wills" this or that. Yet the message that *Kingdom of Heaven* leaves is that individuals *can* rise above the miasma of religious bigotry by plumbing a deeper humaneness that transcends any particular religion. Like other films about the Crusades, *Kingdom of Heaven* does not shy away from depicting the duplicity and depravity of certain crusaders—in this case, the Knights Templar—and the integrity of Saladin. It also finds the theme of romance irresistible but adds a decidedly feminist twist as Sibylla pursues Balian. As in Scott's earlier film *Gladiator,* an intense spirituality underlies the action. Balian at first resists Sibylla as he searches for the meaning of his wife's earlier suicide in France. Jerusalem can provide answers, while Sibylla seems like a distraction. When Sibylla first offers herself to Balian, he refuses, observing that even she, however tempting, is not worth losing his soul for. But they do become involved—emotionally and physically. Sibylla ultimately surrenders the title of queen, an act that clears the way for her lasting relationship with Balian. They return to Balian's village in France to begin anew after their exhausting but liberating involvement in the Crusades.

In the current climate of intense *personal* searches for spiritual meaning, Scott's message resonates with Western audiences. So, too, does its message of religious tolerance. *Kingdom of Heaven* was criticized for its politically correct neutrality and lack of real emotion; that, however, is somewhat harsh criticism as Scott's motive appears to have been depicting the futility of the Crusades by conveying the message that Muslims and Christians *can* resolve conflicts peacefully. In a subtle bow to earlier films about the Third Crusade, at the end of *Kingdom of Heaven,* Richard the Lion-Hearted travels to Balian's French town on the way to Jerusalem. Echoing a line heard earlier in *Kingdom of Heaven,* Balian tells King Richard that to reach Jerusalem, one travels east to where they speak

RICHARD FRANCAVIGLIA

Italian, then continues eastward to where they speak another language. The destination, of course, is the Orient, and we know that Richard will learn as much about himself as he will learn about the place.

The NPR interview with Scott provided a rare look at how a filmmaker depicts history: Scott observed that limited time affects how history is portrayed. As Scott put it, "I can't run a 6½ hour movie, so I've got to telescope; I've got to condense time." Moreover, Scott admitted that "you have to cheat a little; you take certain details which you think are fascinating, and you like to use them with somebody else within this story." Scott here refers to the fact that a filmmaker can justify shifting one deed from one historical character to another as long as that action actually occurred. Scott reiterated that although "there's a little bit of cheating that goes on," the overall effect, if not the historical accuracy, is truthful. This is perhaps another way of stating what religious studies scholar Thomas Martin observed about film. Martin noted that "film has unique powers as a story form" but that "film stories cannot be reduced to analytical written words." To do so would violate, in Martin's words, their "uniqueness." [29] Moreover, in the case of *Kingdom of Heaven*, "the major milestones like the surrender of Jerusalem . . . absolutely did happen that way." [30] Scott's *Kingdom of Heaven* reveals how the Crusades fare in the age of digital special effects. The action—some critics called it an example of Scott's ability to portray "chaotic mayhem" [31]—is intense but probably not overly graphic given the real Crusades' wanton violence. Some critics observed that the flaming projectiles that besiege Jerusalem in Scott's film were not accurate but also acknowledge that this contributed to the battle scenes. It should be noted that all epic battle scenes have forever been shaped by the action in two fairly recent films, *Saving Private Ryan* (1998) and *The Lord of the Rings* trilogy (2001–3). In *Kingdom of Heaven*, the Crusaders' defense of the city of Jerusalem gives one the sense of how potent Saladin's forces are and how withering their punishment of those holding Jerusalem.

The Wind and the Lion

An examination of historically themed films that take place in more modern times demonstrates how Orientalism persists even when filmmakers tackle the fairly recent past. The drama involving abduction of a European (or American) by barbarians has resonated for centuries in captivity narratives. In *The Wind and the Lion* (1975), this theme is central to the plot. The film is based on a historic event—a diplomatic crisis in which a U.S. citizen was kidnapped by a sheik in 1904. This film continues a venerable tradition of casting white males as ethnics, with Scotsman Sean Connery starring as the Moroccan sheik Resuli. Connery's character is by turns brutal and wise—that perfect yin-yang combination that so resonates in Orientalism. We must here recall, however, that the powerful other, whether it be a sheik or an American Indian chief, is usually cast with such ambivalence. He is brutal because he is both a survivor and a leader who has forcefully made his way to the top. He is sensitive and wise because those intelligent traits have enabled him to be revered by his people. The sheik is played by Sean Connery not solely for logistical or racist reasons. Rather, when we look more deeply at the reason our box office idols are cast into such feared/revered roles, we can see that such wise brutes are subliminally *admired* by Hollywood itself. Why? Might it be because they possess the same traits that traditionally characterized successful business leaders?

For his part, the physically fit, bespectacled Teddy Roosevelt, played by veteran actor Brian Keith, represents many of those same male traits that Hollywood finds so appealing. He, too, is a powerful leader associated with both physical prowess (outdoors activity and war) and intelligence (diplomacy, policy). Roosevelt, however, is safely tamed by the democratic process and our knowledge of history into a parental, rather than sexual, being. The Moroccan sheik, of whom we know so little, is a character who fits outside of our historical consciousness and into the deeper folkloric text of mysterious barbarian. Here I would like to make an important observation about Orientalism in the face of civilization. The Oriental despots are not only geographically remote from civilization (i.e., from the East) but are also chronologically remote in that *they represent a different time period, one that is not premodern but "ancient."* In this context, these despots are different from us not solely because they are from exotic places but because they are from a time *before* the flourishing of modern democracies (the late eighteenth century). In our ambivalence, we subconsciously recognize our own roots in this predemocratic tradition of rule by brutal force. This is another way of saying that Orientalism's appeal is based, in part, on Westerners' attraction to a "simpler" time when justice was dispatched not through an elaborate legal process but by swift tribal retribution. This, of course, is a form of primitivism—an "advanced" society finding virtues in the primitive society that it hopes to replace but will inevitably romanticize.[32]

Lawrence of Arabia

In one sense, David Lean's masterpiece, *Lawrence of Arabia* (1962), is the quintessential Old World desert film. It not only renders the desert as almost animate but also resonates with a self-conscious Orientalism. Based on T. E. Lawrence's memoir entitled *Seven Pillars of Wisdom* (published for general circulation in 1935), the film portrays Lawrence's involvement as a British operative in Arabia in 1917. The film is all the more interesting as a cultural statement, however, for Lawrence is both hero and antihero. Ostensibly working for British interests, Lawrence is soon captivated by the power of the desert—and the prospect of a Pan-Arab (rather than British) victory over the despised Turks. These Turks operate almost mechanistically and are reduced to stereotypes. If in *Lawrence of Arabia* some Arabs are treated with respect, the film's Orientalist disdain for the other is revealed in the treatment of the Turks, who are portrayed as barbaric and sadistic. Indeed, one dictionary definition of Turk is someone who is cruel and barbaric—a reflection of how deeply ingrained such stereotypes can become. Ultimately, *Lawrence of Arabia* is literally Orientalist in that Lawrence himself, overwhelmed by his confrontation with the East and its fatalistic way of shaping outcomes, is transformed—both enlightened and beaten down—by the cultural traditions of a land he hopes to transform. The East itself does not change, but rather causes the changing: it transforms individuals, and that is the most significant lesson that Lawrence, and the audience, learn.

No discussion of *Lawrence of Arabia*—both the man T. E. Lawrence and the film about him—can be complete without plumbing Lawrence's deep fascination with the Middle East. Many filmgoers wrongly assumed that Lawrence's military adventures were his first exposure to the region. In fact, Lawrence wrote his undergraduate final examination on "The Influence of the Crusades on European Military Architecture to the End of the Twelfth Century." To do so, Lawrence not only visited castles in Wales, England, and France but also Syria and northern Palestine in 1909.[33] Reading Lawrence's thesis is an eye-opener, for it reveals his fascination with not only military affairs, but his deep appreciation of the Crusader's efforts. One can only imagine the young Lawrence—with notepad, sketchbook, and camera in hand—scurrying over Crusader castles under the blazing sun of a Middle Eastern summer.

However, it is Lawrence as a somewhat more mature young man, but still very much an adventurer and Orientalist, who is immortalized in *Lawrence of Arabia*. Like all antiheroes, Lawrence is conflicted. His anti-Western idealism is emboldened and tempered by confrontation after confrontation. His vision is both brilliant and mad: he hopes to unify the Arab tribes against the Turks, but he confronts three realities: 1) Islamic fatalism, 2) persistent intertribal discord, and 3) British naiveté and deceit. The film's literary and symbolic device—the action is reported by a cynical newsman (in reality the famed journalist Lowell Thomas, but not so named)—is countercultural (that is, aimed at challenging main-

Peter O'Toole (in white) and Omar Sharif in Lawrence of Arabia *(Horizon, 1962; courtesy Photofest)*

stream patriotic assumptions). This is a good example of how Oriental-ism enables one to shift identities—and loyalties. *Lawrence of Arabia* is paradoxically as subversive as it is ethnocentric.

Perceptions about the East's physical environment are important in this process. In *Lawrence of Arabia,* the desert is a powerful mistress.

Lawrence is lured to her but stung by her fickleness—actually the fate that so resonates as fatalism in Islam. As in all historical films, director Lean seizes upon those incidents that tell a story rather than relating events that are purely factual. The swallowing up of an Arab youth by sand, and the killing of an Arab man that Lawrence had earlier saved in defiance of the admonition "it is written," are more metaphorical than absolutely historical/verifiable. These fictional events also underscore the seeming arbitrariness of this part of the world—which can swallow a man and take back a life that had been saved. In the film's finale, Lawrence leaves Arabia a wiser man, but he has paid a very high price. He is burned out, and his idealism is gone. Taken to its ultimate conclusion, Orientalism is self-examination that, if not checked, can become nihilism.

If *Lawrence of Arabia* is among the darkest of Orientalist films, philosophically speaking, it is also the most barren sexually—at least on the surface. There are virtually no women in it, and the only sexuality that does occur involves the rape of Lawrence by a brutal Turkish officer who is fascinated by the whiteness of Lawrence's skin. This event probably never happened, but it represents the penultimate Orientalism at its most negative—brutality without recourse and suffering without redemption. And yet there is another way to view this film: Lawrence's whiteness and his rape transforms him into a female figure who later avenges that degrading act by leading a violent attack against the Turkish forces.[34] Seen thusly, no women are needed in the film because Lawrence himself serves in that feminized role. How else are we to comprehend Lawrence in his headdress and flowing white gown, gazing into the mirrorlike surface of his knife to admire his new look?

Lawrence of Arabia features some of the most stunning desert photography ever recorded on film. This technique juxtaposes the harsh beauty of the environment against the harsh beauty of Islam. It also features some of the truly iconic images of Arabs, including the scene at the well in which a desert sharif (Omar Sharif) rides into the action on a camel in a manner that both confirms his prowess and his barbarism. Sharif shoots an Arab man who is using his well without permission, but Jack Shaheen notes that the scene is pure anti-Arab fiction: an Arab would never commit such an act, as a person in need is never denied. Lawrence's (O'Toole's) bantering with Sharif is a classic in the Western mind confronting the Oriental—and a harbinger of Lawrence's transition into desert warrior. In a sense, Lawrence's (and O'Toole's) going native represents one of the enduring Orientalist questions, even fantasies: what happens when a Westerner loses his (or her) culture and takes on the traits of the native culture? That journey is what makes *Lawrence of Arabia* so enlightening, so terrifying, so mesmerizing—and so Orientalist. It is also what helps make the superb film *Sheltering Sky* (1990)—in which a Western woman voluntarily remains in a harem after her abduction by Arabs—so unsettling and thought-provoking.

Hidalgo

The theme of finding sex and romance in the East is a subtext in the 2004 film *Hidalgo*. Said to be based on the true story of Frank Hopkins, *Hidalgo* pushes the boundary of Orientalism by conflating the deserts of the Old World and the western United States. In *Hidalgo*, Hopkins is part Native American, and jaded—a bit like his aging mustang horse Hidalgo. In a classic test of New World energy confronting Old World cynicism, Hopkins and Hidalgo successfully complete the greatest challenge either has faced—a 1,500-mile race across the Arabian Desert. Their competition, of course, involves real Arabian horses and real—or rather reel—Arabs.

Like most historical films, *Hidalgo* features stylized action, indigenous villains, and romance. Just as any film must be considered in light of the time period in which it was produced, *Hidalgo* must compete with action films—and goes the distance by having Hidalgo outrace a digitized sandstorm. In this regard, the horse race is made more extreme than it actually was. In *Hidalgo*, one gets the impression that the horses actually covered *all* of the mileage, when in the real race they were trans-

Hidalgo *(Touchstone, 2004; courtesy Photofest)*

RICHARD FRANCAVIGLIA

ported over long distances of inhospitable terrain. Also, *Hidalgo* reveals an ongoing obsession with the Middle East. It suggests that the American spirit can triumph here—and show the natives a thing or two in the process. In this regard, *Hidalgo* contains some of the most virulently anti-Arab stereotypes—treachery, deceit, duplicity, cowardice—that tend to mark many American films about the region. And yet films must always be considered in the context of their times. *Hidalgo* was released in 2003. Since September 11, 2001, events in the Middle East have put on shakier ground Shaheen's pre-9/11 claim that Hollywood has absolutely no grounds to "regularly link the Islamic faith with male supremacy, holy war, and acts of terror, [and view] Arab Muslims as hostile alien intruders." Although all can still agree with Shaheen's basic premise that "mindlessly adopted and casually adapted, the Arab-as-enemy stereotype narrows our vision and blurs reality,"[35] *Hidalgo* reminds us that stereotypes are based on broadly shared cultural beliefs, however unfair.

CONCLUSION

Astute readers will note that the number of films about the Crusades is relatively small; after all, only about a dozen or so have been produced in the West in a century. However, it is worth noting that many films subliminally re-enact the Crusades. Some of the more noteworthy include the irreverent *Monty Python and the Holy Grail* (1975), *Raiders of the Lost Ark* (1981), *Indiana Jones and the Last Crusade* (1989), and, more recently, *National Treasure* (2004). These suggest that the Crusades, and Crusaders, are an enduring theme in Western popular culture. The entire event of the Crusades has, in fact, become a trope for Western interaction with the Middle East. With that in mind, we can agree with historian Christopher Tyerman, who, in a recent book about the Crusades, observes and warns: "While it is easy to re-fight the Crusades in modern historical and cultural prejudices, it remains unprofitable if not actually harmful."[36]

The religions of the Middle East are complex, but crusading filmmakers simplify them or, worse, misrepresent them. This is one of the ironies of film, which can capture so much emotion and passion—both positive and negative. As historian of Islamic art Oleg Grabar observes, the Orient of the movie industry (and advertising, for that matter) is "curiously poised between desire and repulsion, beauty and ugliness." It is this ambivalently conceptualized "Orient that answers deep psychological and social needs."[37]

This essay argues that the Crusades endure as one way the West encounters the East. That encounter involves a deeply subconscious memory of loss suffered in the Middle East, and it is one of the operatives in the West's reluctance to surrender this geographic location. That loss occurred in several stages. First, humankind's initial animistic or "pagan" religions were lost to the Judeo-Christian tradition of monotheism and laws governing ethical human behavior: Adam and Eve's ejection from the Garden represents such a loss of the primitive. Second, the Messiah Jesus of Nazareth, who promises eternal life, is inevitably "lost" to the corruption of humanity as Romans and the Jewish authorities crucify him. Third, after the birth and rise of Islam, the actual sites associated with the resurrection are threatened by Muslims who desecrate the Holy Sepulchre—one of the factors that precipitates the First Crusade. Lastly, the loss is deeply metaphorical because the grail is a physical object that, despite being said to possess powers, is ultimately useless, because only *belief* can result in salvation. The loss here is the realization that although no physical possession has any value, the West will defend it at all cost. That angst may help explain the West's ongoing, incessant search for something lost in the East that needs to be recovered.

On film, the Crusades resonate into recent times as a noble search for the Holy Grail, usually in a fictionalized adventure format. Consider again, for example, the popular *Indiana Jones* series of the 1980s, which represents the search for the Holy Grail in the guise of an archaeological adventure story. In the sequel *Indiana Jones and the Last Crusade* (1989), the search for the Holy Grail is explicitly mentioned. The grail's general location is a remote desert area in northern Turkey, more specifically, in the Canyon of the Crescent Moon. That phrase *crescent moon* suggests a connection to Islam. *The Last Crusade*'s story line—that three French templars placed the grail there during the Crusades, but fate caught up with them and they died before it could be retrieved—underscores the perennial search underway. The search for the grail is, according to Jones' professor father (again, Sean Connery), *against* darkness and evil. In *The Last Crusade*, Arabs (or Turks) are not vilified; rather it is the Nazis who are trying to obtain the grail, and if they do, evil will reign. This search for good over evil is enduring enough that yet another sequel of *Indiana Jones* was scheduled for release in 2007.

In *Theology through Film*, Neil P. Hurley observes that there are six rules "that explain why motion pictures are capable of creating intercultural and interfaith bonds among peoples of the world." One of these, a *religious* principle, enables people to "identify negatively with forms of evil and villainy and positively with sacrifice, suffering, and selfless forms of love."[38] That capacity toward universalism, however, can easily be subverted when one religious group uses the negative traits—evil and villainy—to characterize practitioners of another religion. This happens when Christians and Muslims hurl words like *satanic* at each other. Conversely, by using the same principle, religions can characterize their own actions (or the actions of their practitioners or founders) as selfless. It is easy to see why films about conflicts between religions may employ this principle to vilify others and ennoble themselves. Thus, by plumbing moral extremes, screenwriters can fuel intercultural and interfaith hostility. This confirms that film has the power to emotionalize history like no other medium. Action on the screen draws us to it so effectively that it is easy to suspend disbelief—and to even forget history itself—as the dramatized becomes the real.

NOTES

1. One wag even suggested that the ultimate cause of such deaths was not nuclear but rather the gods' way of paying back all involved for making such an awful film.

2. His ultimate martyrdom reaffirms the ultimate sacrifice in a time before martyrdom involved taking as many innocent lives as possible for a religio-political cause.

3. See Robert A. Rosenstone, *Visions of the Past: The Challenge of Film to Our Idea of History* (Cambridge, MA: Harvard University Press, 1995) and Robert B. Toplin, *History by Hollywood: The Use and Abuse of the American Past* (Champaign: University of Illinois Press, 1996).

4. M. A. Muqtedar Khan, *Jihad for Jerusalem: Identity and Strategy in International Relations* (Westport, CT: Praeger, 2004), 104.

5. The term *Turk* has been used for a thousand years; it resonated with Spaniards in the 1500s and likely became even more commonplace as the Ottoman Empire expanded.

6. For an excellent account of the meaning of pilgrimages to Christians, see Craig Bartholomew and Fred Hughes, eds., *Explorations in a Christian Theology of Pilgrimage* (Burlington, VT: Ashgate Publishing Co., 2004).

7. The Catholic Encyclopedia Web site, http://www.newadvent.org/cathen/04543c.htm (accessed 11 February 2005).

8. Khan, *Jihad for Jerusalem*, 107.

9. Dorothy Drummond, *Holy Land, Whose Land? Modern Dilemma, Ancient Roots* (Terre Haute, IN: Fairhurst Press, 2004), 177.

10. Edward Said, *Orientalism* (New York: Vintage, 1979), 1.

11. Ella Shohat, "Gender and Culture of Empire," in Matthew Bernstein and Gaylyn Studlar, eds., *Visions of the East: Orientalism in Film*, 19–66 (New Brunswick, NJ: Rutgers University Press, 1997).

12. Matthew Bernstein, introduction, *Visions of the East*, ed. Bernstein and Studlar, 6.

13. Quoted by Antonia Lant, "The Curse of the Pharaoh," in *Visions of the East*, ed. Bernstein and Studlar, 91.

14. Borges, *Seven Nights*, 48, 51 (New York: New Directions, 1984).

15. Ian Buruma and Avishai Margalit, *Occidentalism: The West in the Eyes of Its Enemies* (New York: Penguin Books, 2004), 146.

16. Weiss, *Translating Orients: Between Ideology and Utopia* (Toronto: University of Toronto Press, 2004), 22.

17. See Buruma and Margalit.

18. See Robert Barry Leal, *Wilderness in the Bible: Toward a Theology of Wilderness* (New York: Peter Lang, 2004).

19. Said, *Orientalism*, 203–4.

20. Weiss, *Translating Orients*, 44–45.

21. S. Caton, Lawrence of Arabia: *A Film's Anthropology* (1999), 5–8 (Berkeley: University of California Press, 1999).

22. Weiss, *Translating Orients*, 170.

23. Weiss, *Translating Orients*, 174–75.

24. Shaheen, *Reel Bad Arabs: How Hollywood Vilifies a People* (New York: Olive Branch Press, 2001) 7, 11.

25. For a treatment of this subject, see Terry Linvall, *The Silents of God: Selected Issues and Documents in Silent American Film and Religion, 1908-1925* (Lanham, MD: The Scarecrow Press, 2001).

26. Robert S. Birchard, *Cecil B. DeMille's Hollywood* (Lexington: University Press of Kentucky), 285–86.

27. Cecil B. DeMille, *The Autobiography of Cecil B. DeMille* (Englewood Cliffs, NJ: Prentice-Hall, 1959), 544.

28. Ridley Scott, interview on *All Things Considered,* National Public Radio, September 11, 2003.

29. Thomas M. Martin, *Images and the Imageless: A Study of Religious Consciousness and Film* (London: Associated University Presses, 1981), 122.

30. Scott interview.

31. Philip Wuntch, "Grail, Grail, the Gang's All Here," *Dallas Morning News,* 6 May 2005, section H.

32. Leah Dilworth, *Imagining Indians in the Southwest: Persistent Visions of a Primitive Past* (Washington, DC: Smithsonian Institution Press, 1996).

33. See Denys Pringle, *Crusader Castles by T. E. Lawrence: A New Edition with Introduction and Notes by Denys Pringle* (Oxford, UK: Clarendon Press, 1990).

34. Shohat, "Gender and Culture of Empire," in *Visions of the East,* ed. Bernstein and Studlar, 19–66.

35. Shaheen, 9, 29.

36. Christopher Tyerman, *Fighting for Christendom: Holy War and the Crusades* (Oxford: Oxford University Press, 2004), preface.

37. Oleg Grabar, "Roots and Others," in *Noble Dreams—Wicked Pleasures: Orientalism in America, 1870-1930,* ed. Holly Edwards (Princeton, NJ: Princeton University Press and the Sterling and Francine Clark Art Institute, 2002), 8.

38. Neil P. Hurley, *Theology through Film,* (New York: Harper & Row, 1970), 5–6.

"THE TRUTH WRAPPED IN A PACKAGE OF LIES"
HOLLYWOOD, HISTORY, AND MARTIN SCORSESE'S *GANGS OF NEW YORK*

••••

DANIEL A. NATHAN, PETER BERG, & ERIN KLEMYK

A much-anticipated and extravagant film, *Gangs of New York* (2002), directed by Martin Scorsese, provides a visually stunning representation of mid-nineteenth-century New York City. Albeit driven by a hackneyed revenge narrative, *Gangs* vividly dramatizes intense, sometimes violent ethnic and class conflicts and the 1863 Draft Riots. The film's mixed critical reception and poor box office receipts must have disappointed its makers, but *Gangs* was widely praised for its gritty evocation of the past. A. O. Scott of the *New York Times* wrote, "There is very little in the history of American cinema to prepare us for the version of American history Mr. Scorsese presents here."[1] Even some academic historians were impressed with aspects of Scorsese's film. Historian Tyler Anbinder, author of *Five Points* (2001), said, "For the specifics, it would get a C. But for the overall theme that the Irish were persecuted and literally had to fight to get their fair share of the American pie, I would give it an A."[2]

We are similarly impressed with some of what Scorsese accomplishes in *Gangs,* especially the film's ability to fire historical imaginations. Thus, this essay critiques *Gangs*'s re-creation of the past. We consider what the film does well in recreating history and what it does poorly. To that end, we have tried to answer the following questions: What kind of historical world does *Gangs* "construct and how does it construct that world? How can we make judgments about that construction? How and what does that historical construction mean to us?"[3]

The questions above are drawn from Robert A. Rosenstone's *Visions of the Past: The Challenge of Film to Our Idea of History* (1995), which has greatly informed our appraisal of *Gangs*. Like Rosenstone and other cultural critics and historians, we think that how Hollywood represents the past is interesting and important. Mark Carnes's *Past Imperfect: History According to the Movies* (1995) and Robert Brent Toplin's *History by Hollywood: The Use and Abuse of the American Past* (1996) and *Reel History: In Defense of Hollywood* (2002) illustrate that this film genre has a long history and that it matters, largely because for many people "Hollywood History is the only history."[4] For us the point is, how should we think about and assess films about the past? What criteria should be applied when "reading" these types of films?

The first thing to keep in mind when thinking critically about a historical film like *Gangs* is that, as Rosenstone argues, it "neither replaces written history nor supplements it. Film stands adjacent to written history, as it does to other forms of dealing with the past such as memory and the oral tradition."[5] Ultimately, Rosenstone suggests, we would be wise to "think of history on film as closer to past forms of history, as a way of dealing with the past that is more like oral history, or history told by bards, or griots in Africa, or history contained in classic epics."[6] As such, critics and historians should not be overly concerned about the "mistakes" or inaccuracies in historical films, or the artistic license filmmakers take with their subjects. These things are to be expected and indeed sometimes encouraged. On its own, the past is usually inert; it needs to be reanimated, hopefully by historically creative, empathetic, and responsible people who understand that their work is always in some sense incomplete. For, as historian Eric Foner reminds us, "there often exists more than one legitimate way of recounting past events."[7] These ideas are particularly germane considering some of the criticism *Gangs* received. One critic, for instance, asserts that the film "purports to be historically accurate" and creates "a new feel-good mythology of the past that replaces the old feel-good mythology."[8]

We think such claims are misguided, and we argue instead that Scorsese's film provides viewers with a complex, multilayered representation of the past that challenges commonly held ideas about the immigrant experience, racism, urban violence, democracy, and history itself. By making these arguments, we are trying to promote a greater appreciation for *Gangs* as a film and, more important, as a valuable work of public history that plays a role in crafting our collective memory and national identity.

Gangs opens in the winter of 1846 with a rumble between the so-called Natives, led by William "Bill the Butcher" Cutting (played by Daniel Day-Lewis) and several gangs of Irish immigrants, led by Priest Vallon (Liam Neeson) of the Dead Rabbits. Each side carries clubs,

Five Points set for Gangs of New York *(Miramax, 2002)*

Engraving of Five Points scene from Valentine's Manual, *1855 (courtesy New York Historical Society*

metal spikes, knives, and chains. The fighting is brutal, leaving the snow-covered ground blood soaked. Ultimately, Cutting kills Vallon—in front of Vallon's young son, Amsterdam—and the Natives win the battle. Bill declares the Dead Rabbits "done and outlawed" and takes control of the Five Points, the densely populated and impoverished lower Manhattan neighborhood one contemporary described as "a perfect hot-bed of physical and moral pestilence."[9] After putting up a fight, Amsterdam is sent to the Hellgate House of Reform.

Flashing forward sixteen years, Amsterdam (Leonardo DiCaprio) returns to Five Points to avenge his father. He quickly learns that Cutting and his gang control the neighborhood and provide Tammany Hall's William "Boss" Tweed (Jim Broadbent) with political muscle. Thanks to a childhood friend, Johnny (Henry Thomas), Amsterdam finds himself "under the wing of the dragon," working for Cutting in various illicit endeavors. The charismatic and vicious Cutting is impressed with Amsterdam's resourcefulness, spirit, and courage, and eventually embraces his protégé as a surrogate son. At the same time, Amsterdam begins a stormy romance with Jenny Everdeane (Cameron Diaz), a "bludget" (female pickpocket) and "turtledove" (house robber posing as a maid) who has an unusual, indeterminate relationship with Cutting. In a moment of jealousy over Jenny's affection, Johnny tells Bill who Amsterdam really is and about his murderous intentions. Shortly thereafter, Amsterdam tries to kill Bill, but his plan goes awry and Bill beats, humiliates, and disfigures him in front of the Five Points community. Jenny nurses Amsterdam back to health, and they resurrect the Dead Rabbits, who align themselves with the Catholic church and the ever-calculating Boss Tweed. Eventually, after several secondary characters (including Johnny) are brutally murdered, the Dead Rabbits formally challenge the Natives to battle. Just before the combatants start to fight, they are interrupted by the Draft Riots, which have spread throughout the city. Despite the commotion, which includes artillery fire from Union warships in the harbor, Bill and Amsterdam clash, and Priest Vallon's son finally gets his revenge. Reunited, Amsterdam and Jenny walk through the city assessing the horrible body count from the riots. The closing shot is of the two lovers staring at the New York City skyline from across the East River. In voice-over, Amsterdam whispers, "It would be like no one even knew that we was ever here."

The plot is not complicated or terribly interesting; it might even be described as clichéd—a third-rate *Hamlet* with a dull love triangle. But as should be clear, we are less concerned with the film's narrative originality than with how it represents the past.

Gangs is embedded in multiple contexts, so beginning with some history is appropriate. The film was made more than thirty years after Scorsese first learned of Herbert Asbury's *Gangs of New York* (1927), a popular history that reads like pulp fiction. Intrigued and inspired by Asbury's book, Scorsese and screenwriter Jay Cocks used parts of it to reflect on some of the people and social forces that created modern New York City.[10] Cocks finished his screenplay in the late 1970s, but the filmmakers could not finance the project.[11] More than twenty years later, bankrolled by Miramax studio, *Gangs* went into production in September 2000, though the revised script was not finished.[12] For myriad reasons, the shooting schedule ran long, from six to eight months, and the movie's release was delayed for more than a year (partly because of the September 11, 2001, terrorist attacks on the World Trade Center). All told, *Gangs* cost approximately $100 million to make, and it finally premiered in late December 2002.[13] Even more than most Hollywood films, *Gangs* experienced tremendous prerelease hype.[14] This was due to Scorsese's well-earned reputation for making gritty, powerful films. And also because *Gangs* features Academy Award–winner Daniel Day-Lewis (after a five-year acting hiatus), Cameron Diaz, and Leonardo DiCaprio, who experienced a wave of intense popularity after starring in *Titanic* (1997), a much more commercially successful (if artistically cautious) historical epic than *Gangs*. Thanks to an aggressive, multimillion-dollar marketing campaign, led by Miramax cochairman Harvey Weinstein, prior to its release *Gangs* "had a 50 percent overall awareness with the audiences it has tested and 64 percent among the much-coveted males older than 18. Such awareness is not surprising given a barrage of international media coverage about the movie."[15] Much of that coverage focused on the "high-volume spats between Scorsese and Weinstein" regarding the shape and length of the film's final cut.[16] "If I could've gotten it down to two hours, I would have," Scorsese explained while promoting the movie. "With this kind of money you owe something to the people who are going to pay for the tickets."[17]

Gangs is a fitting addition to Scorsese's impressive body of work, as many of his films are set in and ostensibly about the city. In fact, *Gangs* is best appreciated within the context of these other movies, which include *Mean Streets* (1972), *Taxi Driver* (1976), *Raging Bull* (1980), an episode from *New York Stories* (1989), *Goodfellas* (1990), *The Age of Innocence* (1993), and *Bringing Out the Dead* (1999), among others. *Gangs* "is the prototype for every one of Scorsese's films," observes film critic Richard Corliss, "it just happens to come after them."[18] Scorsese likewise recognizes that *Gangs* is related to his previous work, explaining that it "represents the foundation upon which all my other movies are based."[19] For example, while most of the gangsters in *Goodfellas* are Italian American, *Gangs* makes it clear that they are the descendents of previous New York criminals, that the city's streets have long been mean, and that violent sociopaths like Jake La Motta and Travis Bickle have historical antecedents.

Yet *Gangs* is historically most closely linked to *The Age of Innocence*, an adaptation of Edith Wharton's 1920 novel of the same title. Set among New York City's social elites, circa 1870, *The Age of Innocence* recounts the ill-fated love affair between the emotionally repressed and conflicted Newland Archer (Daniel Day-Lewis) and the free-spirited Countess Ellen Olenska (Michelle Pfeiffer), a distant cousin of Archer's fiancée, the conventional May Welland (Winona Ryder). Geographically, these characters do not live far from the Five Points, and the Draft Riots would surely be part of their living memory. (One can imagine that Archer was a "$300 man," someone who paid to get out of his military service.) Socially and culturally, however, their lavish world of privilege is far removed from the one that Amsterdam returns to and that Bill the Butcher lords over: one is suffocating in its sumptuousness and rigidity, the other is frighteningly depraved and chaotic. In both cases, though, Scorsese succeeds in transporting viewers into the past, visually and emotionally, via detailed attention to sets and the ways in which his characters walk, talk, dress, eat, and travel.[20] "You feel what it's like to live in this world," says film critic Desson Howe of *The Age of Innocence*, partly because of Scorsese's "fetishistic devotion" to the material world he recreates.[21] Bringing an "anthropologist's view" of nineteenth-century New York upper-class social life, Scorsese is able to explain why his characters, who are just as tribal and almost as vicious as those in *Gangs*, think and act the way they do.[22]

Of course, when thinking about *Gangs* it is also helpful to consider the history of the era it represents. In 1820, there were approximately 130,000 people living in New York City. Over the next forty years, that number would skyrocket to 1 million, as a flood of immigration completely reshaped the city's culture and class distinctions.[23] By 1855, the population of the city's infamous Five Points slum was 72 percent foreign-born, the majority (52 percent) of these recent arrivals from Ireland.[24] Immigrants settling in New York City came from all over Europe.[25] But the potato famine in Ireland was the principal reason driving the masses of Irish to New York City between 1845 and 1850.[26] The immigrants who arrived in New York City and settled in its slums between 1820 and 1860 were greeted with contempt and often violent nativism.[27]

Scorsese skillfully portrays the Irish immigrant experience. One scene depicting a stream of Irish immigrants coming ashore is particularly effective. On one portion of the dock, the immigrants are greeted with warm soup from Tammany Hall representatives, who hope that their generosity will eventually translate into votes. On another, a woman is met with stones from a member of Bill's gang, who shouts, "There's more of that awaiting you in the Points, you Irish bastards." Welcome to the New World.

Actually, *Gangs* has an otherworldly quality to it, which is partly why Scorsese has described *Gangs* as a "Western on Mars."[28] That is, it dramatizes the familiar in an unfamiliar context. The New York City that *Gangs* recreates is comprised of ramshackle buildings of wood and brick, not gleaming skyscrapers of steel and concrete. Scorsese and his team of production designers reconstructed Five Points on a back lot set outside of Rome, at the Cinecittá studio complex.[29] They based their work on nineteenth-century newspaper sketches, engravings, and photographs. On a few occasions, the filmmakers purportedly tried to replicate them almost exactly, as is the case with Jacob Riis's photo "Bandits' Roost," which is recreated in the scene where Amsterdam sells a corpse to medical students.[30] Scorsese says of filming *Gangs:* "I wasn't in Rome. I was at the Five Points, with all the pigs in the street. I was on the set, but in my mind it was real."[31] Indeed, one reviewer argues that the film "has the genius of *thereness* to it."[32] Moreover, several historians appreciate the film's attempts at authenticity. Tyler Anbinder, for instance, notes that Scorsese's portrayal of nineteenth-century New York is visually "just right" and that the filmmakers "couldn't have done much better" in terms of the film's production values.[33] Historian David Henkin adds that the filmmakers recreated Five Points "with considerable thought, research, and expenditure. Gorgeous costuming and sets do an unusually good job of animating the images that have become dull icons for historians of antebellum New York."[34]

Having said that, it is worth stating the obvious: *Gangs* takes many liberties with the historical record. As several historians have documented, some of the film's "mistakes" and inaccuracies are errors of commission (it exaggerates the era's violence), and some are errors of omission (there were many more German than Chinese immigrants in the Five Points). Some are small matters, and some arguably are not.[35] None of this troubles or concerns us; all historical films do likewise. Selection, perhaps even some distortion, is inevitable and is to be expected when projecting the past onto the screen. For pragmatic and aesthetic reasons, filmmakers must manipulate their materials—and they have our cultural permission to do so. Simply put, it is their job. Hollywood filmmakers like Scorsese are primarily storytellers (and business people, obviously). Their responsibilities are artistic and commercial, not scholarly. It is important that moviegoers (and historians) recognize this, that we watch films with our eyes wide open, so to speak.

Besides, some of the liberties Scorsese takes in *Gangs* might be considered fine examples of what Robert Rosenstone describes as "true invention," that is, a representation that, while not literally true, nonetheless "engages the discourse of history" without violating "the overall data and meanings of what we already know of the past."[36] A remarkable instance of Scorsese's ability to compress history into a short, well-

Daniel Day-Lewis as Bill "The Butcher" Cutting in Gangs of New York *(Miramax, 2002)*

crafted scene occurs when some Irish immigrant men walk off the boat wearing their own dingy clothes and thirty steps later are inducted into the Union army and handed uniforms and rifles, just before they are herded onto a ship heading to the war. The camera then pulls back and sweeps across rows of caskets lifted off the very same ship. In the background, an Irish folk song, "Paddy's Lamentation," is sung mourn-

NATHAN, BERG & KLEMYK

fully. After a long, arduous journey across the ocean, these immigrants are met with animosity, conscription, and most likely disfigurement or death. This is not of course literally true; immigrants were not immediately eligible to serve in the military. But it speaks to the tumultuous social world in which immigrants arrived and to the many Irishmen in the Union army.[37]

A common criticism of *Gangs* is that it is gratuitously violent. There is no denying that it is a violent film. Throughout, viewers are provided with images of bloodshed, from Hell-cat Maggie (Cara Seymour) gouging her fortified nails into a Native's face, to Bill the Butcher stabbing a rival in the back with a meat cleaver, to Johnny dying, skewered on an iron fence. Historically, the influx of immigrants into the Points exacerbated long-standing and sometimes violent neighborhood rivalries.[38] With so many different people settling in one place at the same time and struggling to survive, ill feelings and fighting were predictable and common. In fact, though, violent crimes and murder were rare in the Points and did not occur any more often than in other working-class New York City neighborhoods.[39] Still, the Five Points, as Anbinder suggests in his book's subtitle, was "the world's most notorious slum." Vice blanketed the community. Thievery, alcohol abuse, and prostitution were rampant, as the film correctly portrays. Accentuating the neighborhood's violence illuminates the strangeness of a world that seems far off but was pivotal in shaping local and arguably national history and identity. Scorsese frequently mentions the Founding Fathers in interviews, noting their intelligence and sagacity in forming our country's government and political landscape. But, he adds, communities like the Points shaped America's social landscape. As the tagline to the film declares, "America was born in the streets." In other words, though the public infrequently dwells upon it, America arose of "great violence."[40]

Speaking of violence, the film's most intriguing character is Bill the Butcher, played by a virtually unrecognizable Daniel Day-Lewis, who brings an artful "Shakespearean" tone to the film's crass yet charismatic villain.[41] He speaks with a melodic if nasal twang and carries himself with the confidence and grace of a prince, not a butcher in a slum. Attired ostentatiously, in the manner of a man unwittingly parodying his social betters, Day-Lewis aptly describes Bill as a "hooligan dandy."[42] Additionally, Day-Lewis understands that his menacing and mercurial character lives "with a punishing sense of honor, particularly in relation to Priest Vallon, a kind of idealized self who in life and in death confronts Bill with a profound question about his own worth."[43] In perhaps the film's best scene, Cutting, wounded and wrapped in an American flag, describes his penultimate confrontation with Priest Vallon to Amsterdam, not yet aware that he is Vallon's son:

> The Priest and me we lived by the same principles. It was only faith that divided us. He gave me this, you know. [The scar on his face.] That was the finest beating I ever took. My face was pulp. My guts was pierced. My ribs was all mashed up. And when he come to finish me, I couldn't look him in the eye. He spared me, because he wanted me to live in shame. This was a great man. A great man. So I cut out the eye that looked away, and sent it to him wrapped in blue paper. I would have cut them both out if I could have fought him blind. Then I rose back up again with a full heart and buried him in his own blood.

This is a violent man who lives by an archaic code of honor, one so far removed from twentieth-century audiences that only a masterful acting performance can make it accessible. (One historian notes that Bill's code of honor is more medieval than mid-nineteenth century.)[44] Day-Lewis's ability to juggle complexity and brutality creates "a consciously theatrical monster" that film critic David Denby argues holds together the otherwise weak plot.[45]

Bill Cutting, it is worth noting, is loosely based on the historical Bill "the Butcher" Poole, who lived in Five Points in the mid-nineteenth century. An actual butcher and former Bowery Boy gang member, Poole was also a prominent member of the Know-Nothing Party and hated the influx of immigrants, especially the Irish.[46] Like Cutting, Poole was killed by an Irishman; however, Poole died of a gunshot wound after a bar argument in 1855.[47] "He was given a funeral of major proportions, with thousands of mourners," writes Luc Sante in *Low Life: Lures and Snares of Old New York* (1991), an important source for Scorsese's film.[48] Many of those mourners later formed "Poole Associations" dedicated to the preservation of keeping foreigners out of America.[49] Plays were performed that paid homage to Poole in which actors would drape themselves in American flags and repeat his dying words: "Good-bye boys, I die a true American."[50] It is obviously a melodramatic, sentimental farewell, one that Scorsese's Bill the Butcher replicates (minus the "good-bye boys"), but it shows the passion—and irony—with which some nativists held onto their beliefs. Certainly Poole's family originated overseas; the term "native" American is relative.

The film's rendition of Boss Tweed is similarly engaging and maybe more significant. William "Boss" Tweed dominated New York City politics during the mid-nineteenth century from his Tammany Hall office.

He befriended poor immigrants and defrauded the city; estimates range from $50 to $200 million.[51] Tweed successfully maneuvered his way from a school dropout to volunteer firefighter to head of Tammany Hall, stopping in Congress and the state Senate, among other places, along the way.[52] A shrewd, albeit corrupt, politician, Tweed knew how to manipulate and control the city's political system. A large part of Tweed's success came from his ability to connect with poor immigrant voters who were desperate for an ally. Tweed was aware of the needs and concerns of working-class citizens, making clean water available, providing proper sanitation, and improving city streets, and thus garnered their votes.[53] Loved and hated, Tweed found one of his greatest critics in Thomas Nast, a political cartoonist for *Harper's Weekly* at the time, who was disgusted by Tweed's and Tammany Hall's flagrant abuses of power.[54] Ultimately, it was Nast's efforts, in conjunction with a series of *New York Times* exposés, that swayed public opinion and led to the end of Tweed's reign.[55]

Nast's indelible caricatures of Tweed and his Tammany Hall cronies were no doubt on Scorsese's mind when he cast Jim Broadbent to play the politician. With a gray beard, receding hairline, and a portly gut, the film's Tweed owes as much to Nast's cartoons as to the historical record. Despite the cartoonish inspiration, Broadbent's Tweed is not two-dimensional. A respected British character actor, Broadbent skillfully inhabits the role, portraying many of the aspects that made Tweed such a remarkable figure: the cunning wit, shrewd calculation, charm, and cynicism characteristic of many successful American politicians. At Sparrow's Chinese Pagoda, for example, Tweed and one of his Tammany associates observe a card dealer at a fan-tan table. "Know why he wears short sleeves?" Tweed asks rhetorically. "So everyone can see he's got nothing stashed. Jesus, let's hope that never becomes the fashion." When told that the Tammany-backed Irish candidate for sheriff had already won the election by 3,000 more votes than there were voters, Tweed insists that the process continue. "Remember the first rule of politics," he explains. "The ballots don't make the results, the counters make the results, the counters. Keep counting."

At the end of the film, after the city has been through an episode of brutal, widespread violence, Tweed, seemingly overcome by feelings of genuine sorrow at the sight of the dead rioters, says to his Tammany Hall aides, "Tomorrow morning, get our people down to the docks. I want every man and woman coming off the boats given hot soup and bread." After a brief pause, in which it seems as though Tweed feels true sympathy for the dead and the destruction of his city, he adds, "We're burying a lot of votes down here tonight." Staying true to their source until the bitter end, Scorsese and Broadbent refuse to compromise the cynicism

Jim Broadbent as Boss Tweed in Gangs of New York *(Miramax, 2002)*

Boss Tweed, ca. 1860–65 (National Archives)

and political ambitions of the real Tweed for an alternate representation that would have been an unfortunate contrivance.

Probably the film's most important contribution to our understanding of the past is its representation of the Draft Riots, a brutal four-day spasm of violence. The riots were instigated by the federal government's conscription of men who wanted no part of the Civil War and whose anger was partially fueled by racism and class resentments.[56] There had been deadly riots in New York City before the Civil War. Joel Tyler Headley's recently reissued *The Great Riots of New York: 1712–1873* (1873) documents many of them in lurid detail.[57] Still, the Draft Riots were the worst urban uprising in American history and represented something disturbing about many mid-nineteenth-century New Yorkers and their proclivity for violence and mayhem. By all accounts, it was an incredibly bloody and destructive spectacle. According to Tyler Anbinder:

> The predominantly Irish-American mobs lynched a dozen or more African Americans and terrorized thousands. Hundreds of fires were set. Rioters fought pitched battles with the police and the militia for control of uptown avenues. The homes and businesses of prominent Republicans were looted and ransacked. Symbols of federal power in the city also drew the wrath of the enraged populace.[58]

Precise numbers of those killed and injured in the rioting are impossible to document, for the primary sources are contradictory and often unreliable.[59] In this respect, Scorsese gets it right: "How many New Yorkers died that week," says Amsterdam, "we never knew." Like Amsterdam, though, New York survives.

Scorsese's rendition of the Draft Riots is impressive, nearly as vivid, chaotic, and gruesome as the film's opening mêlée. It is depicted via an assortment of "brief, bloody clips interspersed with voice-overs and period drawings."[60] Doing so effectively conveys the bedlam at the heart of the event, the sense that things were spinning out of control and were difficult to comprehend. Just as important, early in the film Scorsese establishes the racial, ethnic, and class tensions that led to the rioting. Immediately after Amsterdam leaves the Hellgate House of Reform, an unreformed young man intent on revenge, we are introduced to the historical moment, 1862. Amid a colorful parade apparently celebrating Abraham Lincoln's Emancipation Proclamation (a banner reads "The President's Proclamation Slavery Abolished In States In Rebellion"), protesters are carrying placards that read "Lincoln Will Make White Men Slaves," "New York Secede From Union," and "Jefferson Davis Our Brother." Immediately thereafter, Cutting sarcastically encourages the marching soldiers, "That's the spirit, boys. Go off and die for your blackie friends." Next, McGloin (Gary Lewis), an Irish immigrant and former Dead Rabbit gang member, assaults an African-American man watching the parade, yelling "Go back to Africa, nigger!" A loud cheer goes up as Cutting expertly throws a knife at a Union Army recruiting poster, hitting an image of Lincoln right between his eyes. In this same scene, Amsterdam explains in voice-over, "The angriest talk was of the new Conscription Act, the first draft in Union history." Later, Scorsese shows a skirmish between a government official documenting who is eligible for the draft and an embittered Irish immigrant who mentions the $300 one needs to be exempted from military service. All of these scenes, and others, help establish meaningful context for the mayhem that is to come.

One could argue that the Draft Riots intrude upon the film's expected conclusion, the confrontation between Bill the Butcher and Amsterdam. Still, much of the critical response to Scorsese's representation of the uprising seems unwarranted. "The images are accurate enough," observes J. Matthew Gallman in the *Journal of American History,*

> but the weight of presentation is distorted and exaggerated, and some of the historical inventions are problematic. We see a few images of African American victims, but the film portrays the riots as a class conflict and underplays the terrible attacks black citizens and institutions suffered, often at the hands of immigrant rioters. Although there was a Union warship anchored near Wall Street, it never bombarded the city. Even if it had, Civil War naval artillery would not have caused the tremendous explosions portrayed in the film. In the movie the riots finally end when fresh, well-drilled Union troops fire into the crowd, an invention that overstates the oppressive power of the federal government. Scorsese's draft riots, like his antebellum riot, are also far bloodier than the real thing.[61]

This is fine criticism, up to a point. Collectively, Gallman's bill of particulars is damning. Taken individually, the merit of each criticism is debatable, not so much as to accuracy, but with regard to its relevance. Surely the naval bombardment can be recognized as a legitimate and effective use of artistic license, one that suggests "the oppressive power of the federal government." More important, the claim that *Gangs* minimizes the attacks on black citizens or that, as David Henkin argues, it inadequately acknowledges "the primary victimization of African Americans" suggests something less than a close viewing of the film.[62]

From beginning to end, Scorsese's version of the Draft Riots depicts African Americans as one of the mob's principal targets. We witness black men beaten, stabbed, and lynched. We hear telegraph operators in voice-over report that "the rioters are attacking colored boardinghouses, robbing them and setting them on fire" and that "blacks are being attacked all over the city." We hear a woman in the crowd yell, "Come on, lads! Kill the nigger bastards! String them up!" *Gangs* represents the Draft Riots as a whirlwind, a frenzy of violence and frustration, but the film does not deny that its foremost victims were African Americans. "The Draft Riots, when all the chips were down, became racial," acknowledges Scorsese.[63]

Predictably, the critical response to *Gangs* is mixed. Some complain about the film's length, well-worn plot, and lack of character development. Others note the film's general inattention to women (especially those who are not gang members, prostitutes, or thieves). Many more praise the film's production values, its "extraordinarily ambitious recreation of a time and place," and Day-Lewis's riveting performance as Bill the Butcher, whom film critic Amy Taubin describes as "ferocious and funny and ultimately tragic—a truly epic creation."[64] But we want to engage a particular criticism of the film and in the process argue that *Gangs*, for all its flaws, is a compelling example of popular culture as public history.

In his essay "Historical Fiction to Historical Fact: *Gangs of New York* and the Whitewashing of History," Benjamin Justice argues that "the film aims for super-realism, right down to the buttons. This emphasis seems to go hand in hand with an unstated assumption about big-budget films: that they are historically truthful."[65] We disagree with this assessment of *Gang*'s intentions and the "unstated assumption" that Hollywood films about the past intend to convey historical truths, at least in the same way that scholarly history books do. For all its attention to period detail and attempts at verisimilitude, *Gangs* is "an impression," Scorsese explains, "a kind of artistic interpretation."[66] In a different interview, Scorsese is even more explicit: *Gangs* "is based on history. There is no doubt about it. But it is still a film that is more of an opera than history."[67] Given the film's melodrama and gore, one would be wise to take Scorsese's disclaimer seriously, to recognize that "the film laces history with poetic fire."[68] Furthermore, viewers need to remember Amsterdam's very first words, spoken retrospectively in voice-over: "Some of it I half remember. And the rest . . . the rest I took from dreams." This should be read as an admission that the narrative that follows should not be taken literally. Like most feature films about the past, *Gangs* does not make bold claims about its historical veracity. (And even if it did, one should be critical of them.)

At the same time, Justice correctly notes that *Gangs* will probably "become a major source of the public's understanding of the past."[69] For good and for ill. Its portrayal of the Irish immigrant experience, the Five Points, and the Draft Riots is visceral, not veracious. The film does not reflect the latest historical scholarship nor aspire to the cool detachment of a documentary film series like Ric Burns's *New York* (1999). Rather, it conveys a sense of the mid-nineteenth century's disorder and menace, the ways in which different kinds of New Yorkers (natives and immigrants, Protestants and Catholics, socially elite and working-class men) lived and struggled with each other, politically and physically. Yes, its representation of the past is often melodramatic and manipulative. But *Gangs* has historical value nevertheless. It vividly dramatizes some of the complex, bitter struggles immigrants faced when they reached the New World, even if it romanticizes the righteousness of some Irishmen. Equally important, it presents a disunified Union; few enough contemporary Americans have heard of the Draft Riots, let alone considered the fact that not all northerners at the time were in favor of fighting the Civil War. *Gang*'s greatest accomplishment, however, is its emotional force, its ability to communicate the texture and furor of the past, or at least something akin to it.

In this way, *Gangs* is part of an important tradition, related to other epic American films like *The Birth of a Nation* (1915), *Gone with the Wind* (1939), *JFK* (1991), and *Saving Private Ryan* (1998). The aforementioned are, we recognize, historically flawed and politically charged films; many people find some of them noxious. They are also compelling examples of the ways in which popular culture texts can entertain and educate (or propagandize, depending on one's perspective). The connections and differences between *Birth* and *Gangs* are particularly noteworthy. Separated by nearly eighty years, both films are based on popular books, are visually spectacular, and try to explain the mid-nineteenth-century origins of modern America. D. W. Griffith's melodrama about the Civil War and Reconstruction—which sympathizes with beleaguered white southerners; vilifies so-called radical Republicans, carpetbaggers, and scalawags; caricatures (and frequently demonizes) African Americans; and reconciles the North and South via a shared sense of white supremacy—was a tremendous commercial and critical success.[70] *Gangs* was not; for example, its take at the domestic box office was less than the film cost to make.[71]

Nonetheless, some critics and historians recognize and appreciate its connection to *Birth*. A. O. Scott notes that *Gangs* self-consciously conjures the memory of *Birth*, which "is one of the targets of Mr. Scorsese's revisionism."[72] More specifically, the film's representation of the Draft Riots, Scott argues, signals "the catastrophic birth of a modern society. Like the old order, the new one is riven by class resentment, racism and political hypocrisy." Impressed with Scorsese's "bravery and integrity," Scott concludes that *Gangs* provides viewers with an "unsparing and uncompromised imagining of the past," though it is not always pleasant

NATHAN, BERG & KLEMYK

Martin Scorsese directs Cameron Diaz (Jenny Everdeane) and Leonardo DiCaprio (Amsterdam Vallon) in Gangs of New York *(Miramax, 2002)*

to watch or contemplate. Taking a different, less admiring tack, historian Timothy J. Gilfoyle suggests that both *Birth* and *Gangs* are "structured around a conception of the past grounded in myth" rather than solid history.[73] Gilfoyle notes that *Gangs* conveys "a blood-soaked vision" of the American past, rather than a sanitized one, but that ultimately Scorsese's film, like *Birth*, is "another mythic, cinematic epic disguised as nineteenth-century history."[74] One might convincingly argue that *Birth* masqueraded as history, as Griffith aspired to make a "historically honest movie" and consistently maintained that he had, much to the annoyance of many African Americans and historians.[75] It is a great deal more difficult to make the same case for *Gangs*. Scorsese clearly envisions his narrative in operatic terms and acknowledges that his film is, at best, "the truth wrapped in a package of lies."[76]

Gangs is not *the* truth, of course, as if there was only one. On the contrary, a careful reading of the film and history supports the idea that mid-nineteenth-century New York City was awash in competing truths, that it was, as historian Thomas Bender puts it, "a place of multiple realities and partial comprehensions."[77] What Scorsese succeeds in doing is representing some of those grim realities and imperfect comprehensions. He temporarily transports moviegoers to an unfamiliar place and time that had an impact on shaping the here and now. It is a textured world, atmospheric, incredibly vibrant, and, yes, exaggerated, but not to the point of historical absurdity. Like many artists (novelists, playwrights, and painters, for example) who take the past as their subject, Scorsese attempted to craft a coherent (perhaps even didactic) narrative out of a historically complex moment rife with unpleasantness and indeterminacy. And as a Hollywood filmmaker, he had the extra burden of producing a commercially viable work. Moreover, as someone with a rich sense of cinematic history, Scorsese understands that in Hollywood "one iron rule remains true: every decision is shaped by the money men's perception of what the audience wants."[78] As a pragmatist, Scorsese knows that he "is in the business of telling stories," stories that need to satisfy different audiences.[79] Reflecting on *Gangs*, Scorsese explained: "With a budget of $96 million or something you have to be responsible for that money. So you have to try to combine what interests you with some elements of box office and some responsibility to the studio."[80] Juggling multiple responsibilities—artistic, historical, and commercial—is very difficult, which may account for some of the film's shortcomings and disappointments. If nothing else, though, the movie and its maker need to be appreciated for their ambition. For besides capturing the contentious, chaotic nature of mid-nineteenth-century New York City, Scorsese's *Gangs* encourages viewers to think critically about the past and to participate in conversations about Hollywood's portrayal of history and how memory functions.

NOTES

It is with great pleasure that we thank Greg Pfitzer and Elliott Gorn for their constructive criticism, Skidmore College's Faculty/Student Collaborative Research Program for supporting our work, and John Brueggemann and Chuck Joseph for going above and beyond on our behalf.

1. A. O. Scott, "To Feel a City Seethe as Modernity Is Born," *New York Times*, 20 December 2002, E35.

2. Interview on *All Things Considered*, National Public Radio, 23 December 2002.

3. Robert A. Rosenstone, *Visions of the Past: The Challenge of Film to Our Idea of History* (Cambridge: Harvard University Press, 1995), 50.

4. Mark C. Carnes, "Introduction," *Past Imperfect: History According to the Movies*, ed. Mark C. Carnes (New York: Henry Holt and Company, Inc., 1995), 9.

5. Rosenstone, *Visions of the Past*, 77.

6. Ibid., 78.

7. Eric Foner, *Who Owns History?: Rethinking the Past in a Changing World* (New York: Hill and Wang, 2003), xvii.

8. Benjamin Justice, "Historical Fiction to Historical Fact: *Gangs of New York* and the Whitewashing of History," *Social Education* 67 (May/June 2002): 214.

9. Quoted in Tyler Anbinder, *Five Points: The 19th-Century New York City Neighborhood That Invented Tap Dance, Stole Elections, and Became the World's Most Notorious Slum* (2001; New York: Plume, 2002), 1.

10. Martin Scorsese, Gangs of New York: *Making the Movie* (New York: Miramax Books, 2002), 19–20.

11. Kevin Baker, "'You Have to Give a Sense of What People Wanted,'" *American Heritage*, November/December 2001, 50, 52.

12. Josh Young, "Ready to Rumble," *Entertainment Weekly*, 24 May 2002.

13. Ibid.

14. Dana Harris and Cathy Dunkley, "Miramax, Scorsese Gang Up," *Variety*, 14–20 December 2001, 38.

15. Laura Holson, "Miramax Blinks, and a Double DiCaprio Vanishes," *New York Times*, 11 October 2002, C1.

16. Young, "Ready to Rumble." According to one journalist, "Scorsese was Patton to Harvey Weinstein's Truman, but by most accounts the genius general in the trenches won the battles he needed to win." Timothy Rhys, "Martin Scorsese's Comfortable State of Anxiety," *MovieMaker* http://www.moviemaker.com/issues/48/scorsese.html (21 January 2005).

17. Young, "Ready to Rumble."

18. Richard Corliss, "Have a Very Leo Noel," *Time*, 23 December 2002, 66.

19. Interview on *All Things Considered*, National Public Radio, 23 December 2002.

20. Jim Koch, "Filming Edith Wharton's World: You Were How You Ate," *New York Times*, 15 September 1993, C3.

21. Desson Howe, "Scorsese Does 'Age' Well," *Washington Post*, 17 September 1993, N52.

22. Vincent Canby, "Grand Passions and Good Manners," *New York Times*, 17 September 1993, C1.

23. Howard Zinn, *A People's History of the United States: 1492-Present* (New York: HarperCollins Publishers, 1995), 213.

24. Anbinder, *Five Points*, 43.

25. Ibid., 43.

26. Ibid.

27. Zinn, *A People's History of the United States*, 222, 230.

28. Amy Taubin, "Founding Fathers," *Film Comment*, January/February 2003, 25.

29. Luc Sante, "The Fabrication," *New York Times Magazine*, 12 November 2000, 114. *Gangs* reportedly cost $90 million to make, partly because the set on which it was filmed "is one of the most remarkable ever constructed. On a one hundred-acre back lot outside of Rome, set designer Dante Ferretti spent six months rebuilding much of lower Manhattan. We're talking no less than forty-five life-sized buildings inspired by original floor plans and grainy daguerreotypes. To ensure authenticity, Ferretti even imported bricks from New York." Bryan Mealer, "Gangs of New York," *Esquire*, October 2001, 148.

30. Baker, "'You Have to Give a Sense of What People Wanted,'" 54.

31. Ibid., 54–55.

32. Stephen Hunter, "A Bloodied Past," *Washington Post*, 20 December 2002, C1.

33. Interview on *All Things Considered*, National Public Radio, 23 December 2002.

34. David Henkin, review of *Gangs of New York*, *American Historical Review* 108 (April 2003): 620.

35. J. Matthew Gallman, review of *Gangs of New York*, *Journal of American History* 90, no. 3 (December 2003): 1125; Timothy J. Gilfoyle, "Scorsese's *Gangs of New York*: Why Myth Matters," *Journal of Urban History* 29, no. 5 (July 2003): 622–25; Henkin, review of *Gangs of New York*, 620.

36. Rosenstone, *Visions of the Past*, 72, 79.

37. Edward K. Spann, "Union Green: The Irish Community and the Civil War," in *The New York Irish*, ed. Ronald H. Bayor and Timothy J. Meagher (Baltimore: Johns Hopkins University Press, 1996), 193.

38. Elliott J. Gorn, "'Good-Bye Boys, I Die a True American': Homicide, Nativism, and Working-Class Culture in Antebellum New York City," *Journal of American History* 74, no. 2 (September 1987): 410.

39. Anbinder, *Five Points*, 225, 233.

40. Baker, "'You Have to Give a Sense of What People Wanted,'" 54.

41. Scott, "To Feel a City Seethe," E35.

42. Scorsese, Gangs of New York: *Making the Movie*, 61.

43. Ibid., 63.

44. Gilfoyle, "Scorsese's *Gangs of New York*," 624–25.

45. David Denby, "For the Love of Fighting," *New Yorker*, 23 December 2002, 166.

46. Gorn, "'Good-Bye Boys, I Die a True American,'" 395.

47. Ibid., 389.

48. Luc Sante, *Low Life: Lures and Snares of Old New York* (1991; New York: Vintage Departures, 1992), 259.

49. Gorn, "'Good-Bye Boys, I Die a True American,'" 391.

50. Ibid., 392.

51. Leo Hershkowitz, *Tweed's New York* (New York: Anchor Press/Doubleday, 1977), xv.

52. Allen J. Shire, "Tweed, William M(agear) 'Boss,'" in *The Encyclopedia of New York*, ed. Kenneth T. Jackson (New Haven: Yale University Press, 1995), 1205.

53. Jonathan Kandell, "Boss," *Smithsonian Magazine*, February 2002, 86–87.

54. Shire, "Tweed," 1206.

55. Ibid.

56. Iver Bernstein, *The New York City Draft Riots: Their Significance for American Society and Politics in the Age of the Civil War* (New York: Oxford University Press, 1990); Edward K. Spann, *Gotham at War: New York City, 1860–1865* (Wilmington, DE: SR Books), 93–105.

57. Joel Tyler Headley, *The Great Riots of New York: 1712–1873* (1873; New York: Thunder's Mouth Press, 2004).

58. Anbinder, *Five Points*, 314.

59. Spann, *Gotham at War*, 101.

60. Gallman, review of *Gangs of New York*, 1125.

61. Ibid.

62. Henkin, review of *Gangs of New York*, 621.

63. Baker, "'You Have to Give a Sense of What People Wanted,'" 52.

64. Peter N. Chumo II, "Gangs of New York," in *Magill's Cinema Annual 2003*, ed. Christine Tomassini (Farmington Hills, MI: Gale Group, Inc., 2003), 175; Taubin, "Founding Fathers," 26.

65. Justice, "Historical Fiction to Historical Fact," 213.

66. Baker, "'You Have to Give a Sense of What People Wanted,'" 56.

67. Interview on *All Things Considered*, National Public Radio, 23 Dec. 2002.

68. Peter Travers, review of *Gangs of New York*, *Rolling Stone*, 24 July 2003, 101.

69. Justice, "Historical Fiction to Historical Fact," 214.

70. Robert Lang, ed., *The Birth of a Nation: D. W. Griffith, Director* (New Brunswick, NJ: Rutgers University Press, 1994), 171; Fred Silva, ed., *Focus on Birth of a Nation* (Englewood Cliffs, NJ: Prentice-Hall, Inc., 1971), 1.

71. One source says that *Gang*'s box office was $37.9 million. Chumo, "Gangs of New York," 174. Another indicates that it grossed more than $77 million in the United States and close to $200 million worldwide. See http://www.imdb.com/title/tt0217505/business.html (21 January 2005).

72. Scott, "To Feel a City Seethe," E35.

73. Gilfoyle, "Scorsese's *Gangs of New York*," 626.

74. Ibid., 621, 627.

75. Bruce Chadwick, *The Reel Civil War: Mythmaking in American Film* (New York: Alfred A. Knopf, 2001), 121, 126.

76. Baker, "'You Have to Give a Sense of What People Wanted,'" 56.

77. *New York: A Documentary Film, Order and Disorder, Episode Two: 1825–1865*, prod. Lisa Ades and Ric Burns, dir. Ric Burns (Steeplechase Films, 1999).

78. *A Personal Journey with Martin Scorsese through American Movies*, prod. Florence Dauman, dir. Martin Scorsese and Michael Henry Wilson (1995; A BFI TV Production for Channel 4 in association with Miramax Films, 2003).

79. Ibid.

80. Rhys, "Martin Scorsese's Comfortable State of Anxiety."

IN DEFENSE OF THE FILMMAKERS

····

ROBERT BRENT TOPLIN

When traveling to Dallas to deliver the Webb Lectures at the University of Texas at Arlington, I engaged in a conversation about film and history at a Washington, D.C. airport that seemed quite familiar to me. A woman who was also waiting for the plane to Dallas asked me why I was traveling to Texas, and I indicated that I was going to speak at UT-Arlington about the way Hollywood movies deal with history. After making a few complimentary remarks about the university, the woman offered some personal comments on the subject of my lecture. She guessed that I would enjoy criticizing Hollywood moviemakers for making a wreck of history. "Don't they do a terrible job?" she asked. The woman encouraged me to lambaste Hollywood artists for manipulating and distorting evidence. She expressed concern that impressionable young Americans were gaining mistaken impressions about history from Hollywood artists who cared mostly about profits, not education.

As I mentioned at the beginning of my book *Reel History: In Defense of Hollywood,* I hear similar complaints frequently when individuals offer their first thoughts about the relationship of motion pictures to the public's understanding of the past. Most commentators assume that Hollywood is bad for history. Like the woman who scolded moviemakers in my brief discussion at Washington's Dulles airport, they assume that movie audiences will discover little of value when they watch a popular film about a historical subject. If the film has any impact on viewers, they conclude, that influence must be negative rather than positive.

I would like to challenge this dark picture of Hollywood's relationship to historical interpretation. As I mentioned to the audience at

Titanic *(Paramount, 1997; courtesy Photofest)*

UT–Arlington, I went to Texas not to bury Hollywood but to praise it. That praise should be tempered, however, by an appreciation of film's limits. Obviously, Hollywood feature films cannot deliver fully satisfactory historical insights. Movies cannot perform all of the instructional services that books, articles, or lectures provide. Their shortcomings should be acknowledged and discussed. Yet we can also recognize that motion pictures can stir the thinking of audiences in useful and, indeed, different ways. Cinema does not address historical questions in the same manner that traditional forms of communication do. It does not communicate insights in the style of a published work or a speech. Once we recognize the distinctions, however, some of Hollywood's contributions should come into clearer view.

Movies that interpret history do not represent the most popular genre among the many types that are popular with today's moviegoers. Theater and home video audiences display far greater interest in viewing films categorized as action/adventure movies, comedies, romances, horror films, and other genres. Not many historical movies appear at neighborhood theaters or video rental stores each year in comparison with the other entertainment categories. History-oriented pictures are in short supply not only because of the audience's tastes but also because of cost. Cinematic history is usually expensive. While a filmmaker can put together a clever satire such as *Sideways* (2004) and realize large profits on the basis of a relatively small investment, producing a historical movie usually involves much greater financial risk. Those productions

ROBERT BRENT TOPLIN

often call for period costumes, old-looking buildings, and many other period props. When viewing a depiction of history on the big screen, patrons expect to see a big-scale epic film such as *Lawrence of Arabia* or *Gladiator.*

They anticipate viewing panoramic scenes that require huge sets and hundreds of extras. When that kind of epic succeeds, as in the case of James Cameron's *Titanic,* millions of movie lovers will acclaim the filmmaker's splendid achievement. When such movies fail to attract critical attention and large audiences, as in the case of *Heaven's Gate,* the experience can prove very painful for both the creative personnel that designed the film and the Hollywood executives that backed it with millions of dollars.

Despite the obvious problems and risks, historical pictures continue to emerge each year, and often they win the greatest critical acclaim of all the genres. Consider the films nominated each year as Best Picture. Motion pictures with stories set in the past are usually among the nominees. Often these films take the top prize, the Academy Award. Since the 1980s, most of the movies that received the Oscar were, broadly speaking, examples of historical cinema. These films interpreted the past. Their stories were set in the past. The list includes movies such as *Gandhi, Chariots of Fire, Platoon, Driving Miss Daisy, Dances with Wolves, Schindler's List, Braveheart, The Unforgiven, The English Patient, Titanic,* and *Shakespeare in Love.*

Do these historical films affect audiences' thinking about the past? Do these movies leave viewers with impressions about the lessons of their own times? A recent news story indicates that viewers do sometimes think about such lessons. The report indicated that some Palestinian leaders were screening Richard Attenborough's 1982 classic, *Gandhi,* for fellow organizers involved in the struggle with Israel. The Palestinian promoters of *Gandhi* thought that their cohorts could learn some valuable lessons from watching the Academy Award–winning drama about the Indian leader's struggle to win independence for his country from Britain.

Mahatma Gandhi practiced peaceful means of protest and succeeded marvelously in embarrassing the British soldiers and inspiring worldwide sympathy for the independence cause. The movie's Palestinian promoters hoped that the screening would provide a useful model of successful protest for dealing with Israel's dominance in the West Bank and Gaza.

Another interesting example of the impact of Hollywood movies on audiences relates to *Saving Private Ryan* (1998). Steven Spielberg's film provided a powerful stimulus to public interest in the history of World

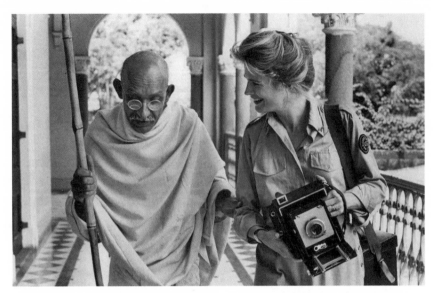

Ben Kingsley as Mahatma Gandhi and Candice Bergen as Life *photographer Margaret Bourke-White* (Gandhi, *Sony Pictures, 1982; courtesy Photofest*)

War II. Tours of beaches along the coast of Normandy where Allied forces invaded the mainland of Europe in June 1944 became especially popular with tourists after the appearance of *Saving Private Ryan.* Visitors wanted to see locations depicted in the popular film that starred Tom Hanks. The movie also boosted sales of books about D-Day and its aftermath written by Stephen Ambrose, the popular historian who had served as an adviser to Spielberg's movie project. Spielberg, in turn, drew many of the details for his portrayals from two books by Ambrose, *D-Day* and *Citizen Soldiers.* In fact, *Saving Private Ryan* helped spike a general return of book readers and moviegoers to themes related to the Second World War. Before long, NBC News anchor Tom Brokaw was successfully promoting his book of veterans' reminiscences, *The Greatest Generation,* and television producers were preparing a multipart drama based on Ambrose's writings.

Titanic also made a "splash," by arousing audiences' curiosity. James Cameron's 1997 epic, which broke all sales records for a Hollywood movie, aroused tremendous public interest in the historical record of the ill-fated voyage of 1912. When the movie first appeared in theaters, America's bookstores were filled with publications dealing with the historic event. Readers displayed a voracious appetite for books about the voyage and sinking of the *Titanic.* Later, a traveling exhibit of museum artifacts drawn from the sunken *Titanic* made its way around the United

ROBERT BRENT TOPLIN

Saving Private Ryan *(Dreamworks, 1997)*

States and attracted large crowds of curious onlookers. Audiences expressed so much interest in the ship that some business investors talked about building a new *Titanic* with interiors that looked like those on the original vessel. They thought travelers would be delighted to take vacations on an ocean liner that resembled the historic ship and the movie's vessel. Probably many travelers would be eager to step out on the bow in the manner of the romantic couple in Cameron's film, Jack and Rose, or they would want to walk up the ship's great staircase and see the famous clock displayed in the movie.

Some films appear to have made a notably positive impact on audiences. For instance, *Holocaust,* a multipart drama made in Hollywood for television, appears to have provoked a useful interest in the history of one of the twentieth century's greatest tragedies. The movie communicated a story about two families that knew each other in prewar Germany (one was Jewish, the other Nazi) and followed their activities through the World War II years. When NBC broadcast the series in the United States in 1978, the program drew large and enthusiastic audiences. Many Americans praised the TV series as a sort of Jewish *Roots* (referring to ABC's *Roots,* the tremendously popular 1977 television drama that portrayed American slavery from the slaves' point of view). More importantly, *Holocaust* became tremendously influential in Europe, attracting huge audiences. The reception in Germany was particularly interesting. At first German television authorities did not want to broadcast the series. They called it superficial and dismissed the production as soap opera from Hollywood.[1] Eventually, however, some of the German subsidiary stations carried the program, and those broadcasts provoked a tremendous audience response. Millions of Germans followed the story on television, and thousands wrote letters to the television stations asking why German schools had failed to teach the history of the Holocaust. These writers also wanted to know if German citizens had been aware of the atrocities during World War II. Shortly after the program's broadcast, German scholars became deeply involved in a lively debate about their nation's handling of stories about the Holocaust. NBC's movie helped to bring examination of Nazi Germany's tragic history into the open.[2]

Many years later, the Jewish movie director, Steven Spielberg, traveled to Germany to promote his own movie about the Holocaust, *Schindler's List* (1993) and received a hero's welcome. Leading figures in the newly unified country attended the movie's premier and praised Spielberg for portraying the sensitive and controversial topic of genocide with great sophistication. German authorities also brought Oskar Schindler's wife to their country (she had been living in Argentina) and honored her.[3] A later incident in Switzerland showed how *Schindler's List* could make an emotional impact on a viewer. A guard working in a Swiss bank saw piles of papers in the basement that were scheduled to be destroyed. When he examined the documents, he recognized that they were records of accounts held in the bank years before by Jewish victims of the Holocaust.

The guard reported the situation to the Swiss authorities. When members of the press asked him what had moved him to call the authorities, he said he remembered the faces of the people in *Schindler's List*. That movie inspired him to take action.[4]

While *Holocaust* and *Schindler's List* represent positive examples of the impact of historical movies, there are also examples of unfortunate influences. The case of *The Birth of a Nation* has especially attracted attention from historians and students of film as an illustration of the genre's negative influence. D. W. Griffith's 1915 movie was, in a sense, the first Hollywood blockbuster. At considerable expense (for its time), the long film depicted the American Civil War and the Reconstruction period in the postwar South. Based on a novel by North Carolinian Thomas Dixon, *Birth of a Nation* provided a positive view of the Ku Klux Klan's activities in the South after the war and portrayed African Americans in quite negative ways.

When the film appeared in Boston, New York, and Los Angeles, it aroused considerable protest. Critics warned that the emotion-laden story could set back race relations in the United States.[5] Indirectly, that appears to have occurred. When some white Georgians heard that *Birth*

Schindler's List *(Universal, 1993; courtesy Photofest)*

Birth of a Nation *(Image Entertainment, 1915; courtesy Photofest)*

of a Nation was soon to appear in Atlanta, they held a ceremony on Stone Mountain on the outskirts of Atlanta and reorganized the Klan, which had been dormant for decades. Soon after the film's showing, many white southerners joined the reconstituted Klan. Organizational activity then spread into the North, the Midwest, and the West. By the 1920s millions of Americans participated in Klan activities. *Birth of a Nation* had helped to stimulate initial interest in this organization that based much of its appeal on contempt for racial, ethnic, and religious minorities.[6]

We find another questionable example of Hollywood's apparent influence on attitudes and behavior in the case of the 1970 Academy Award winner for Best Picture, *Patton*. Franklin Schaffner's biopic portrayed George S. Patton during World War II, with George C. Scott performing a memorable impersonation of the famous and controversial soldier. Schaffner and others who crafted the movie intended to present a two-sided perspective on the general, one that was both positive and negative in its characterization. The filmmakers portrayed Patton to be an amazingly talented leader but also one who loved war so much that he sometimes appeared dangerous or unbalanced. Richard M. Nixon, president of the United States when Schaffner's movie was released, came away from the film viewing experience with only one part of the intended message, the positive image. Nixon thought General Patton was exactly the kind of tough-minded leader America needed in a time of war. President Nixon had his own problems with war-making at the time that he viewed *Patton*. The Vietnam conflict was proving tremendously difficult for American troops, and Nixon was trying to decide whether to expand that military engagement into the neighboring country of Cambodia. Viewing *Patton* helped give him the courage to act: he asked key advisers in the White House to view the movie, and he called for the U.S. invasion of Cambodia.[7] His decision to expand the fighting beyond Vietnam was tremendously controversial. Students on college campuses across the United States protested loudly. The situation became especially volatile in Ohio, where the governor sent National Guard troops onto the campus of Kent State University. The soldiers carried loaded weapons, and after a few days of angry exchanges between students and the Guard, troops fired a quick burst of gunshots that left four young people dead and several wounded. Months after the shocking Kent State incident, Nixon pulled U.S. and South Vietnamese troops out of Cambodia. The situation in Cambodia later slipped into chaos and violence as the radical followers of dictator Pol Pot took advantage of these dislocations and seized control of the society. Within a few years, millions of Cambodians were dead because of the harsh policies of Pol Pot and his fanatical supporters. Obviously, Schaffner's movie, *Patton*, cannot be blamed for all of these tragic developments, but the motion picture seems to have made some small contribution to the course of history by inspiring Nixon's call for the invasion of Cambodia.

While Hollywood movies sometimes seem to influence specific behaviors, often their impact appears to be more general. Films may affect the American people's broad perceptions of the past. Consider, for example, the way movies about the past provide the images that Americans typically conjure in their minds when imagining scenes from history. Ask young Americans to picture life in the days of ancient Rome, and they may draw upon images from *Gladiator* (2000). Older citizens may think of scenes from the 1950s sword-and-sandals epics such as *The Robe* (1953) or *Ben Hur* (1959). If Americans are asked to imagine life in the historic Old West, older citizens may recall scenes from John Wayne movies, while younger ones may draw upon images from Clint Eastwood's movies (or from the surly characters in HBO's recent hit, *Deadwood*). When Americans picture World War II, they often draw upon Hollywood images, too. Older citizens are likely to look again to a John Wayne film, perhaps a classic such as *The Sands of Iwo Jima* (1949). Younger moviegoers are likely to draw upon memories of more recent productions such as *Saving Private Ryan* (1998).

These images stay locked in our memory banks because dramas about the past have a tremendous emotional impact on us. Movies help us to think about the past not in terms of dry statistics but in terms of the flesh and blood characters we have seen *experiencing* history on the screen. Authors and playwrights have long understood the power of dramatic fiction for making history come alive. Shakespeare delighted audiences centuries ago with historical fiction about Julius Caesar and the English kings. Tolstoy provided a memorable story about Napoleon's actions in *War and Peace*. Margaret Mitchell told an influential tale about the Old South in *Gone with the Wind* (and, of course, the story later came to movie screens in a blockbuster film). The prolific author, James Michener, delivered history to millions of readers through his tremendously popular fiction about people and events in Hawaii, Alaska, Poland, and other places. Dramas and historical fiction from these authors excited the public's interest in history. As with movie treatments of the past, their artistry could not give readers a full story about history and certainly not an "accurate" one. Nevertheless, their productions could stimulate the public's curiosity and excite audiences' interest in learning more about the subjects addressed in drama and fiction.

Before I elaborate on the related contributions of historical film, it is first important to recognize some of cinema's obvious shortcomings. In the course of praising Hollywood filmmakers for arousing audiences to think about the past, we can easily overlook many problems associated with the historical genre. I do not want to be accused of "irrational exuberance." Before proceeding with a defense of history by Hollywood, I should identify some of the most glaring difficulties that need attention. Five problems with cinematic history stand out particularly, and it would be easy to add many other complaints to this list were we to devote chapters rather than pages to this discussion.

First, movies tend to favor the "great person" approach to history. Secondly, dramatic films usually depict specific events rather than explore big ideas or offer broad analyses. Thirdly, historical movies do not ordinarily offer comprehensive views of the past. They leave out a great deal. Fourthly, the movies frequently present one-sided rather than multi-sided perspectives. Finally, dramatic films about history, at least the Hollywood variety, deal disproportionately with stories about war.

In the early nineteenth century, the Scottish historian Thomas Carlyle wrote about the great man theory of history (with an emphasis on heroes); we can update that observation to include great women as well. Followers of this school of interpretation tend to focus on the activities of extraordinarily talented, motivated, and courageous people. These "movers and shakers" from history change the problems they encounter by imposing the force of their dynamic personalities upon them. Moviemakers typically follow this approach to interpretation in their films. Director Steven Soderbergh, for instance, portrayed a humble file clerk, with a mission to protect citizens from dangerous pollution, taking on a powerful electric company and winning in his hit movie *Erin Brockovich* (2000). In that example of cinematic history and in many others, a tremendously driven individual presses for change and ultimately enjoys remarkable achievements.

We know, however, that individuals cannot alone move mountains. Their achievements in pressing for changes depend, to a large degree, on conditions of the times. Unfortunately, movies rarely give audiences much appreciation of these background factors. If Hollywood made a new drama tomorrow that focused on John F. Kennedy's success in winning the presidency in 1960, the director would likely portray Kennedy as a man of extraordinary political gifts. This imagined film would probably give attention to JFK's good looks, his attractive family, and his eloquent manner of speech. In short, Hollywood would make the election success appear to be almost solely the consequence of one man's unusual talents and drive.

Historians know, however, that a sophisticated discussion of the political events of 1960 ought to move beyond recognition of one man's extraordinary skills. Among the many factors a historian must consider in analyzing Kennedy's election victory is religion. A few decades before 1960 a Catholic candidate would likely have fared poorly in a national campaign for the White House (as the Democratic candidate Al Smith did in 1928) since Protestants dominated the political scene in the United States. By 1960, however, many Catholics were second- or third-generation American, and the religious issue had become less significant in the national elections. Kennedy's Catholic affiliation was a factor but certainly not as big an element as it would have been years before. Thus, the professional historians' judgments about Kennedy in 1960 would have to take into account many elements, including changes in the American public's attitudes toward religion. The filmmakers' approach to the story would likely promote the idea that a "great man" succeeded in winning an election largely from his own energy and drive.

A second shortcoming of most history-oriented movies pertains to the absence of big ideas and broad analyses. While some authors of historical studies ponder big questions through intriguing analyses, filmmakers very rarely engage in such activity in the course of depicting history on-screen. To be sure, some filmmakers are intelligent and informed about diverse subjects, and they manage to communicate a *few* of their thoughts in subtle ways through portrayals in their movies. But these filmmakers can hardly provide a direct philosophical discussion in their popular dramas, and they cannot engage big ideas in the fashion that some skilled historians are able to do in sophisticated treatises. Recognizing this shortcoming does not suggest, necessarily, that movies offer nothing of value. This observation only identifies a contribution that books and lectures tend to deliver more effectively than dramatic films.

Consider the achievements of *Saving Private Ryan,* a movie that received much critical acclaim. Did Steven Spielberg's memorable drama about soldiers' experiences during the period of the Normandy invasion of 1944 tell audiences much about why the United States entered World War II? Did it explain why many Americans of 1944 considered the Nazis evil and desperately wanted to see them defeated? Did the movie explain how the United States won the war in Europe? Did it throw light on the strategies employed by American and German generals in the armed confrontations on the shores of France in 1944? Obviously, we must respond in the negative to all of these questions. *Saving Private Ryan* was a terrific movie, but its gifts to audiences did not involve the presentation of insightful expositions on broad questions that call for detailed and complex interpretations. The movie provoked thought but not in ways that might be achieved in an informed and insightful written treatment of the subject.

A third major example of the shortcomings of historical cinema concerns the tight focus of most of these dramas. Cinematic history must simplify and symbolize complex information so that audiences will understand its stories and take a strong interest in them. Real history, as opposed to reel history, is often complicated, contradictory, and confusing. If filmmakers attempted to portray events in exact sequence and with portrayals of all the principal figures that were involved in the actual events, their productions would probably never receive financing from the studios. If by some miracle their movies did receive the necessary monetary support, they would probably become box office flops. Audiences can easily feel lost if they cannot clearly understand a movie's story or empathize with the individual characters in it. That is why moviemakers typically compress the time in which events take place (making a number of developments appear to happen within a short period). Filmmakers frequently collapse several individuals from history into a few key characters to facilitate the audience's understanding. In fact, Hollywood storytellers often project one key individual on the screen, making that heroic figure stand in for several different people from the past. Benjamin Martin (Mel Gibson), the invented hero of *The Patriot*, served that purpose for a story about the coming of America's Revolutionary War. Most importantly, filmmakers leave out many events to tighten their storytelling. Critics of historical cinema often fail to appreciate this requirement for the crafting of drama. They complain that artists left out a significant battle, gave no attention to an important speech, or did not include a friend or relative that was a significant figure in the real historical figure's life. Film reviewers should not be surprised that much material is omitted. Entertaining and successful historical cinema requires such simplification and creative license.

A fourth shortcoming of cinematic history relates to perspective. History from Hollywood usually comes in the form of one-sided interpretations of the past that focus on a clash between heroes and villains. A right and wrong position is assigned to each major issue addressed in the movies, and apparently no screen time is available for key characters that stand between the extremes. Filmmakers address practical and moral choices in stark terms. In a fundamental way their interpretations are one-dimensional. When scholars address historical questions in writing and lectures, however, they often explore two, three, or more possible answers to a question. The scholar may note that there is disagreement among professionals on the relevant controversies and then discuss each of the prominent explanations. The professional historian may eventually take a position in this debate about interpretation but only after examining a variety of choices. Filmmakers tend to choose one interpretation of events and hammer it continuously.

Mel Gibson's *Braveheart* represents an excellent example of this Hollywood approach. *Braveheart* depicted a conflict between the Scots and the English in terms of good and evil, white and black. There were few gray areas in the story. Early in the film audiences see that the hero, played by Mel Gibson, lives happily among his fellow Scots. Then the evil English appear in the story, bringing misery to their Scottish victims. These early scenes help audiences understand why the movie's hero will seek revenge and freedom for his compatriots. Not every cinematic history presents the issues in terms as stark as *Braveheart*, but certainly most movie dramas approximate this storytelling strategy. The makers of dramatic film tend to define right and wrong in clear ways.

How many big-budget Hollywood epics can we identify that do not employ this strategy? Which major historical movies introduced audiences to several different interpretations of a subject and challenged viewers to make individual judgments about which explanation appears to be most truthful? We would have difficulty naming many major films that interpreted the past with such complexity.[8]

This shortcoming is serious, because debates about interpretation are at the center of the professional historian's work. Controversies about history and clashes of interpretation make the study of the past interesting and relevant. A good deal of professional scholarship involves efforts to contribute new information and new insights to old debates. We call these disputes about the meaning and lessons of the past "historiography," and much of our energy in research goes into the pursuit of new and alternative contributions to it. The Hollywood movie often fails us, because it rarely introduces audiences to the debates that animate historians.

Finally, as has become especially obvious in recent years, cinematic history deals disproportionately with armed conflict. Big-budget movies about the past are usually about war. The notable cinema of recent years has depicted battles between the Scots and the English, the American Patriots and British Regulars, the Texans and the Mexicans, the Yankees and Confederates, the Americans and Nazis, the Americans and the Japanese, and the Americans and the Vietnamese. War is interesting and certainly exciting when it is portrayed on the big screen, but there is much more to history than war. Many important subjects from the past deserve the attention of Hollywood's artists, but these stories never reach the screens of neighborhood theaters, because the historic situations available for depiction do not involve armies, navies, and air forces. Certainly war stories can provide opportunities to address significant ideas and issues, but the range of analytical possibilities is considerably narrowed when filmmakers must channel their depictions of people's disagreements through portrayals of armed conflict.

This problem of the dominance of war stories has become especially acute in recent years because of the increasingly international character of Hollywood's marketing activities. Years ago, Hollywood earned most of its profits from domestic sales, but these days more than 60 percent of a movie's earnings may come from the sales overseas of tickets at the box office, videos, and DVDs. This is especially true of the big historical epics. *Troy* (2004), for instance, cost a great deal to produce, but it was not especially popular with American audiences or American critics. Yet *Troy* played well abroad and racked up huge profits.

Filmmakers turn especially to war stories when depicting history, because action represents an international language. Audiences in the Philippines or Brazil or Egypt may not understand or appreciate the subtleties of language and culture employed in a Hollywood comedy or serious drama, but they can easily understand the elements of a war story and enjoy watching the clash of hundreds of soldiers in deadly combat. War sells well around the world, and now it appears that Hollywood is turning almost exclusively to it when gambling on an expensive historical epic.

A review of these five principal shortcomings of cinematic history might lead some observers to dismiss Hollywood's productions as simple minded and generally worthless entertainment. After all, these movies appear to offer quite limited outlooks on the past. They typically provide the great man and great woman approach to interpretation instead of sophisticated analyses of the diverse factors that influence societies. Movies rarely examine big ideas. They are usually not as comprehensive in their treatments of historical subjects as books, and they fail to address the big debates about interpretation that interest professional historians. Instead, movies usually deliver one-sided interpretations. Furthermore, they give primacy to war stories, missing many important opportunities for commenting on the human condition.

There is much that disappoints in historical cinema, yet a summary dismissal of these productions as mindless entertainment seems a rather severe and simplistic conclusion. While traditional modes of historical interpretation (through books and speeches) provide much of value to audiences, films, too, can contribute to the public's appreciation of history. These contributions are delivered in a different manner, however. We will not recognize film's value if we apply the same standards to its evaluation that we apply to a book or a lecture about history. Film communicates in distinctive ways, and to appreciate its impact on audiences we need to consider a distinctive vision.

Movies about the past often provide an emotional hook that pulls audience interest toward a study of the subject. Cinematic history may fall

Braveheart *(Paramount, 1995)*

short in terms of presenting statistics and factual details about events, but it often excites the viewers' curiosity. Drama on the big screen can draw audience sympathies toward the travails of a story's main characters. By making viewers think emotionally about the experiences of William Wallace, Mel Gibson's character in *Braveheart*, the movie aroused audience concern and stirred curiosity. Many viewers left the theaters eager to read about the history of Scotland, particularly the Scots' troubles with the English.[9] The Irish and Welsh found the story inspiring, too, for it suggested ideas about their own appeals for the devolution of English political power. Indeed, most popular Hollywood epics work in this fashion. By engaging the audience's sympathies for principal characters, these movies arouse a hunger for greater knowledge about the historical context. That is why bookstores displayed numerous titles about the *Titanic* in 1997 and World War II in 1998 (after the appearance of *Titanic* and *Saving Private Ryan*).

The case of *Saving Private Ryan* suggests another quality of cinematic history: movies give audiences a *feeling* for life in a distant time and place. University-based history professors work arduously to achieve this goal in their classrooms. They attempt to give what one scholar calls a sense of the "pastness of the past." Instructors sometimes introduce paintings, photographs, music, news film, recorded interviews, and a variety of other sources of information to help students develop an emotional appreciation for conditions of life in an earlier time and a different place.

Communicating such a "feeling" was one of Steven Spielberg's distinctive accomplishments in directing *Saving Private Ryan*. Scenes from the first half hour of the movie are especially memorable. Students who wonder what the experience of combat was like during World War II received a striking presentation on the subject from Spielberg. The director cleverly provoked an emotional sense of the dangers soldiers faced by making his depiction look like newsreel footage. Spielberg washed out much of the color in his print so that his movie looked somewhat like a black-and-white film. Through use of the hand-held camera, he arranged for cinematographers to run with the actors who were playing soldiers that charged up the beaches, another technique that made the movie look like newsreel footage. Then, by featuring loud and realistic-sounding explosions and images of mangled bodies and limbs flying in the air, *Saving Private Ryan* gave audiences a powerful sense of the frightening and horrible experiences of the soldiers who joined the first waves of attacks at Omaha Beach. Perhaps better than any book, the movie aroused an emotional connection to that historic situation of long ago. After watching the movie, viewers better understood why the G.I.s' assault was so difficult. Small facts about the attack, such as information about panicked soldiers, immobilized units, and desperate efforts to scale the nearby cliffs, become more meaningful in the context of the movie's emotion-laden depictions.

I was tremendously impressed with the emotional power of *Saving Private Ryan* when I first saw it in New York City in connection with an appearance on The History Channel. After watching the preview in a small theater with members of the national media, I was curious about audience reactions in neighborhood theaters around the country. To examine the reactions on a small scale, I viewed *Saving Private Ryan* again when it appeared at a theater near my home in Wilmington, North Carolina. The impact on audiences was fascinating. When the movie came to an end and the credits rolled on the screen, hundreds of patrons walked out of the theater silently. Usually patrons are eager to share thoughts with friends or family members at the conclusion of a movie. They discuss favorite scenes, render judgments about the movie's merits, or comment on the actors' performances. At the conclusion of *Saving Private Ryan*, however, no one in the theater seemed eager to talk. Spielberg's salute to the fallen soldiers of World War II was so powerful that it appeared inappropriate to speak under the circumstances. To engage in typical post-movie chatter in the first minutes after the film's conclusion seemed like dishonoring the men who lost their lives in World War II.

ROBERT BRENT TOPLIN

Many commentators on film will acknowledge that movies deliver a powerful emotional kick, but they complain that Hollywood filmmakers do not present "accurate" pictures of the past. These critics say Hollywood artists "make up" too much of the history they project on the screen. Filmmakers invent scenes, note the critics. They create characters that didn't really live in history and manipulate details to make their productions entertaining, the critics note. Why don't the creators of these dramas simply replicate the *real* history of the times, these complainers ask. Truth, they insist, is much more interesting than fiction.

Accurate strikes me as a troublesome and inappropriate word to employ in these discussions about cinematic history. Our discussions about film would profit greatly if we generally set this term aside, since it is not truly applicable to the task of the filmmaker. Movies cannot be "accurate" in their portrayals, because filmmakers do not have access to all of the small details of historic situations. They do not know exactly how people looked and sounded. Nor do scholars. Historians and filmmakers know little of what the people in history said and did behind closed doors—in private situations. Much of the historic record is the public record. It shows how individuals delivered a major speech or acted in a public event. Sometimes filmmakers and historians rely on private letters for information, yet even these documents provide limited insights into the questions that intrigue scholars. It is always difficult to be "accurate" in reporting on a historic figure's motivations, feelings, interests, goals, and purposes. People who interpret the past in print or film speculate on these matters. With only fragments of information at their disposal, they try to offer educated guesses about what happened and why.

Interestingly, filmmakers must be quite clear about this speculation, while traditional historians are in a much better position to remain noncommittal in their exercises in speculation. Scholars can render judgments in complex ways. They often cite many different explanations for events (a condition addressed earlier), and frequently they end a discussion by rendering a qualified judgment that may be weakened by a presentation of evidence that contradicts the principal thesis. Some scholars eschew firm judgments. They deliver information that offers many different perspectives on a historical question and let the reader decide which of the many proposed explanations seems to provide the more truthful conclusion. Filmmakers cannot utilize such opportunities for evasiveness. Every decision they make in creating a movie drama takes them in the direction of presenting a forceful interpretation.[10] The details in each scene must almost always communicate a strong-minded interpretation. One character in a scene may appear pretty, sincere, and genuine. She may be dressed in attractive clothing and speak warmly and sympathetically to another figure in the story. Perhaps that other individual represents the "heavy" in this imagined motion picture. She is somewhat sinister looking, and her voice is deeper than the heroine's. To communicate villainy, the director may employ some telltale Hollywood signs. Perhaps the "heavy" will be seen smoking a cigarette, drinking heavily, or cursing profusely. Cinematography may contribute to this communication as well. In *Schindler's List,* for example, Steven Spielberg and his cinematographer, Janusz Kaminski, delivered interpretations in every image. They threw light and shadows on principal characters, placed their cameras low when shooting pictures of the hero (Liam Neeson as Oskar Schindler) to make him appear tall and impressive, and employed numerous other techniques that influenced the audiences' judgments about the story. The cinematography of Spielberg and Kaminski also conspired to make the key Nazi in their story (played by Ralph Fiennes) blatantly evil. In appearance, mannerisms, tone of speech, and other elements of presentation, Fiennes played a despicable character. If the filmmakers had not designed their scenes in this heavy-handed manner, they would have left audiences confused and, possibly, disinterested.[11]

In short, the "truth" about people and situations from history is often a subject of complex debate among historians, but filmmakers must project a particular vision of "truth" in every frame of a movie. The specific nature of dramatic film requires such opinionated renderings. Productions with big budgets are far more likely to succeed at the box office if they communicate specific visions of right and wrong, good and bad, progress and regression. If a movie does not succeed in delivering this strong vision, it will likely sink into obscurity, despite otherwise impressive attributes.

Ride with the Devil represents a striking example of this problem. The sophisticated 1999 movie directed by Ang Lee depicts violent clashes in the borderland regions of Kansas and Missouri during the American Civil War. *Ride with the Devil* offered many well-researched depictions of life in those troubled times, yet the movie did not communicate a clear vision of its thesis, and the characters in each scene were not always clearly assigned to heroism or villainy. The story left many viewers confused, and it failed to attract much public interest when it appeared in neighborhood theaters. This otherwise fine film sank quickly into obscurity. *Ride with the Devil*'s disappointingly short run in the theaters showed the difficulty filmmakers face when they try to turn away from conventions of the cinematic genre. The rules of drama are familiar to Hollywood artists and studio executives for a fundamental reason: they have stood the test of time. Over the years, audiences have responded much more favorably to films that have employed familiar techniques of cinematic history. Movies that challenge those traditions boldly, such as *Ride With the Devil,* hardly draw notice.

While many critics of cinematic history agree with my recommendation to put aside demands for accuracy, quite a few critics remain insistent that Hollywood's interpretations of the past tell the "truth." Whether a film deals with the Civil War or women's suffrage or a close election contest in history, commentators often argue that they want the movie to reflect reality and not distort and manipulate the historical record. This interest in defending truthful cinematic histories is commendable, but we should acknowledge that we can never be sure that we are in possession of a completely objective interpretation of the past. Virtually every action that we take in an effort to make sense of history involves an exercise in personal judgment. As historians and filmmakers, we find a messy, confusing, and incomplete record from the past in the archives. A lot of important information is missing. As interpreters, we must decide which of the few fragments from the past (the available "facts") we will privilege and bring forward for our audiences' consideration. Then we must connect those selected "facts" in an argument that is supported with words, pictures, music, and other elements.[12] This entire exercise called "interpretation" requires judgments. Interpreters of the past may strive for objectivity, but it is difficult to bless their entire operations as impressively objective descriptions of the past. Each interpreter brings emotional and intellectual baggage to the study of history. Often the interpreter does not recognize the subtle influences on his or her perceptions. Whether the historian or filmmaker is American, European, or Asian may make a difference in the judgments rendered about historical facts. The interpreter's religious affiliation (or lack of it) can make an impact. The political ideology of the storyteller is relevant, too. In short, it is difficult to demand that movies tell the truth when no historical interpretation, not even one presented in a well-researched book, can be certified as the essential truth.

It is useful to move from the abstract to the particular when discussing this challenge of searching for truths. Consider some of the most familiar controversial subjects from recent American history. Whether we provide answers to tough questions by means of a book or a movie, personal judgments are essential. Commentators do not simply communicate the acknowledged truth. For instance, what is the objective truth about the following controversies? Did President Harry Truman take the wise and moral course of action when he decided that the United States would drop atomic bombs on two Japanese cities near the end of World War II? Was the United States right or wrong about the decision to intervene extensively in the affairs of Vietnam? The answers depend to a large degree on one's political perspective. What is the truthful and objective judgment about the leadership of President Bill Clinton? Students writing term papers about Clinton's years in the White House might come up with very different responses, because they would select and stress different "facts" when framing their answer. Some might think that the evidence of a tremendous economic boom in the Clinton years suggests the appropriateness of a very positive conclusion. Others would reach a strongly negative conclusion by stressing evidence about Clinton's romantic affairs and denial of them under oath. Some future historians will likely praise President George W. Bush for demonstrating firm convictions during his years in the White House and advancing the conservative cause, while others will criticize him severely for leading the country into a questionable war in Iraq and squandering the nation's budget surplus. Truth seems always a matter of contention among historians. We should not be surprised, then, that filmmakers often join these debates about the past, too, and that they render very strong judgments about truth because of the fundamental nature of drama.

Critics of the movies sometimes become so finicky about details and "accuracy" that they miss the filmmakers' larger contribution. These critics fail to recognize that some degree of manipulation is inherent in filmmaking, and sometimes that exercise of artistic license can serve a useful and defensible purpose. A Hollywood artist may adjust small details about a historical situation in order to draw the audience's attention to an important subject that needs serious consideration. In these situations the artist may sacrifice some small truths in order to communicate larger ones. Robert A. Rosenstone and I have often referred to the example of Edward Zwick's *Glory* (1989) to illustrate this point. Zwick's movie focuses on the experiences of African American military recruits during the American Civil War. In real life the Massachusetts regiment depicted in the film was made up largely of free black men from the North. Zwick portrays the unit as represented largely by former slaves who achieved their emancipation during the war. This distortion of the specific facts does not deeply trouble James M. McPherson, one of the nation's prominent Civil War scholars. McPherson judges Zwick's manipulation of facts understandable and defensible to an extent, because it achieves a useful purpose. Since many thousands of black soldiers that fought for the Union were, indeed, former slaves, Zwick gave movie audiences an appreciation of this little-known information from the history of the war. The director (and the screenwriter, Kevin Jarre) manipulated a small "truth" in order to advance understanding of an important larger "truth." McPherson considers this exercise of artistic license defensible.

ROBERT BRENT TOPLIN

Glory *(Sony Pictures, 1989; courtesy Photofest)*

He recognizes the value of *Glory* as a powerful commentary on history, and he considers the movie to be truthful in large ways even if it is not always "accurate" in its treatment of small details.[13]

When considering Hollywood's record of producing numerous influential films about the past, students of history need to demonstrate a modern understanding of the diverse ways that movies communicate interpretations. The moviemakers' mode of presenting history is, of necessity, very different from the manner in which scholars and teachers present history in books or in classroom lectures. Movies can arouse an audience's curiosity about the past, and this contribution deserves greater public attention. Far too many scholars and teachers (as well as citizens operating outside of the academy) discuss film in a way that suggests that they expect movies to deliver comprehensive interpretations of major historical problems. Film can never do that, especially Hollywood productions that depict the past in a dramatic format. Yet, as we have seen, the public is often aroused by provocative cinematic treatments of historical subjects. Popular movies about personalities and past events often boost book sales. These films can excite students' interest in conducting research on related subjects. Students are more likely to participate in animated discussions about historical topics once they see them depicted in intriguing portrayals on the big screen.

Hollywood movies do not bring closure to discussions about history. But they do have the potential to open them. When popular movies are viewed in this manner, the familiar complaint that cinema gives young people the wrong ideas about history seems irrelevant. Stories in motion pictures should never be treated as the last word on a subject. They should be considered useful aids for raising questions and launching informed and insightful discussions about the past.

NOTES

1. John Vinocur, "'Holocaust' TV Series Criticized, Is Sidelined by West Germans," *New York Times*, 3 July 1978, 2.

2. "'Holocaust' Audience Far Bigger than West Germans Anticipated," *New York Times*, 25 January 1979; Ellen Lentz, "Effects of 'Holocaust' on West German TV Cross Border into East," *New York Times*, 28 January 1979, 11; Charles R. Maier, *The Unmasterable Past: History, Holocaust, and German National Identity* (Cambridge, MA: Harvard University Press, 1988), 1–8, 44, 47–56, 118.

3. Liliane Weissberg, "The Tale of a Good German: Reflections on the German Reception of Schindler's List," in Yosefa Loshitzky, *Spielberg's Holocaust: Critical Perspectives on Schindler's List* (Bloomington: Indiana University Press, 1997), 177–78, 184.

4. "Swiss Bank Guard Seeks Asylum in U.S.," *Wilmington* (N.C.) *Star-News*, 21 May 1997, 1.

5. A good review of the debates can be found in Fred Silva, ed., *Focus on* Birth of a Nation (Englewood Cliffs, NJ: Prentice-Hall, 1971).

6. David Mark Chalmers, *Hooded Americanism: The First Century of the Ku Klux Klan, 1865-1956* (Garden City, NY: Doubleday, 1965), 25-32; Kenneth T. Jackson, *The Ku Klux Klan in the City, 1915-1930* (New York: Oxford University Press, 1967), 3-4. For a discussion about the movie's quality as a film and its unfortunate message about race relations, see William Grimes, "Can a Film Be Both Racist and a Classic?" *New York Times,* 27 April 1994, B1.

7. I review the case of Nixon's reactions in Robert Brent Toplin, *History By Hollywood: The Use and Abuse of the American Past* (Champaign: University of Illinois Press, 1996).

8. I explore these traditions of Hollywood storytelling in the historical genre in Robert Brent Toplin, *Reel History: In Defense of Hollywood* (Lawrence, KS: University Press of Kansas, 2002), 23-30.

9. Colin McArthur, "Braveheart and the Scottish Aesthetic Dementia," in *Screening the Past: Film and the Representation of History,* ed. Tony Barta (Westport, CT: Praeger, 1998), 180-81.

10. Robert A. Rosenstone, *Visions of the Past: The Challenge of Film to Our Idea of History* (Cambridge, MA: Harvard University Press, 1995), 67-69.

11. Toplin, *Reel History,* 50-52.

12. Hayden White discusses these issues in "The Modernist Event," in *The Persistence of History: Cinema, Television, and the Modern Event,* ed. Vivian Sobchack (New York: Routledge, 1996), 17-32. Also, see Hayden White, "Historigraphy and Historiophoty," *American Historical Review,* December 1988, 1193-99. White develops a broader notion of these ideas in *The Content of the Form: Narrative Discourse and Historical Representation* (Baltimore: Johns Hopkins University Press, 1987) and *Tropics of Discourse: Essays on Cultural Criticism* (Baltimore: Johns Hopkins University Press, 1978).

13. James M. McPherson, "The 'Glory' Story," *The New Republic,* 8 and 15 January 1990, 22-27. McPherson also examines the film in Mark C. Carnes, ed. *Past Imperfect: History According to the Movies* (New York: H. Holt, 1995), 128-31.

ABOUT THE CONTRIBUTORS

A proud Minnesotan and graduate of Skidmore College, PETER BERG is interested in film criticism and history, contemporary literature, and creative writing.

RICHARD FRANCAVIGLIA is Professor of History and Geography at the University of Texas at Arlington and has a special interest in how places have been depicted in popular culture, including maps, literature, music, and film. He serves as director of UTA's Center for Greater Southwestern Studies and the History of Cartography, and his geographic specialty is the world's arid regions.

ERIN KLEMYK is a graduate of Skidmore College and teaches English and creative writing at Watkinson School in Hartford, Connecticut.

The author of *Saying It's So: A Cultural History of the Black Sox Scandal* (2003), DANIEL A. NATHAN is an Associate Professor of American Studies at Skidmore College, where he teaches courses on twentieth-century cultural history, including a class that examines how Hollywood filmmakers represent the past.

GEOFF PINGREE is Associate Professor of Cinema Studies and English at Oberlin College. An independent writer, photographer, and documentary filmmaker, he regularly depicts culture and politics in Spain for academic and public audiences.

PETER C. ROLLINS, Oklahoma State University, is Editor-in-Chief of *Film & History: An Interdisciplinary Journal of Film and Television Studies,* www.filmandhistory.org. In 2006 two of his books received the Ray and Pat Browne Award of the Popular Culture/American Culture Associations: *The Columbia Companion to American History on Film* and *Hollywood's West: The American Frontier in Film, Television, and History.*

ROBERT ROSENSTONE is Professor of History at the California Institute of Technology and the author of several book-length works of history, biography, and criticism, including most recently *King of Odessa* (2003) and *The Man Who Swam into History* (2005). He created the first film section of the *American Historical Review,* and he is the founding editor of *Rethinking History: The Journal of Theory and Practice.* He has been involved as consultant or writer on several film projects including *Reds, The Good Fight, Darrow,* and *Tango of Slaves.* Rosenstone has been awarded four scholarships by the National Endowment for the Humanities and three from the Fulbright program, and has been a research fellow at both the East-West Center (Honolulu) and the Getty Research Institute.

ROBERT BRENT TOPLIN is Professor of History at the University of North Carolina at Wilmington and the author or editor of a dozen books. His latest books include *Reel History: In Defense of Hollywood* (2002) and *Michael Moore's* Fahrenheit 9/11: *How One Film Divided a Nation* (2006). Toplin has also served as a commentator on film and history on several nationally broadcast television and radio programs.